**MANUALIA DIDACTICA 16
UNISA 1991**

AFRICAN TRADITIONAL RELIGIONS

An introduction

S A Thorpe

UNIVERSITY OF SOUTH AFRICA
PRETORIA

© 1991 University of South Africa
First edition, first impression
Second impression 1992
Third impression 1993

ISBN 0 86981 732 9

Printed and bound by Sigma Press, Koedoespoort

Published by the
  University of South Africa
  P O Box 392, 0001 Pretoria

© All rights reserved. No part of this publication may be reproduced in any form or by any means – mechanical or electronic, including recordings or tape recording and photocopying – without the prior permission of the publisher, excluding fair quotations for purposes of research or review.

Contents

Preface   vii

Chapter 1   Introduction   1

Chapter 2   The elusive San   9

   Historical and cultural review   9
   The religious orientation of the San   16
      Mythology   16
      The Bushman concept of God   21
      Dance, trance and health   24
      Religion and the community   25
      Religion and the environment   28

Chapter 3   The Zulu people of Natal   30

   Historical review   30
   Cultural review   32
   The religious orientation of the Zulu people   34
      Belief in a supreme sky god   35
      The extended community   38

Chapter 4   The Shona-speaking people of Zimbabwe   49

   Historical review   49
   Cultural review   52
   The religious orientation of the Shona people   54
      Belief in Mwari   54
      Belief in a spirit realm   56
      Belief in good and bad medicine   58
      Belief in the continuing community   62
      Marriage customs   63
      Death customs   64

Chapter 5 The Mbuti pygmies 67

    Historical and cultural review 67
    The religious orientation of the Mbuti 74
        Socio-ethical relationships 74
        Conceptions of divinity 78
        Religious rituals 80

Chapter 6 The Yoruba of West Africa 84

    Historical review 84
    Cultural review 86
    The religious orientation of the Yoruba people 89
        Olorun/Olodumare 89
        The orisha 91
        Ancestral spirits and secret societies 95
        The Ifa divination system 97
        Priests, prayers and places of worship 99
        Birth, marriage and death 101

Chapter 7 The African pattern 104

    A Supreme Being 108
    Societal harmony and well-being 110
        Societal disruption 113
        Religious authorities 114
        Rites and rituals 117

Epilogue African religions and the future 118

    Community solidarity 119
    Rituals 120
    Symbolism 121
    Traditional versus Western doctors 122
    Temporal orientation 123

Works consulted 126

Preface

Although there are a number of excellent anthropological and ethnographical accounts available which touch upon the religious orientation of African peoples, not a great deal has been written from a strictly religious perspective. Books such as those by Mbiti, J S 1975. *Introduction to African religions*, and Taylor, J.V. 1963. *The primal vision*, are not only out-of-print but tend to treat African religions generically, not giving attention to the individual systems in which the various phenomena find their home. Although King (1970) gives more attention to the variety of systems present in Africa, his book *Religions of Africa* is no longer in print. *African cosmos* (1986) is available, but King, by his own admission, is weak on southern African religions, which is precisely where I wish to place the greatest emphasis. This state of affairs was brought to my attention when I searched for material that could serve as a textbook for first year university students who wished to begin a study of African religions. It is for this reason that I have written the present work.

A number of books have been listed at the end of each chapter as 'suggested reading'. In many instances these books were useful in the preparation of the material within that chapter. With respect to the core chapters the books generally represent authors who are recognised authorities in the area of study for which they are indicated. In chapters 1 and 7 this is not necessarily the case. Although Ray (1976), for example, has largely relied on the research of others in the preparation of his book, it nevertheless presents a perspective on African traditional religion which is worthy of note. I do not wish to endorse everything presented in the books listed for 'suggested reading' but I think that they can give additional information to those who aim to pursue further the issues presented in the relevant chapters.

This book has been written with the conviction that African traditional religions deserve our attention in that they have something of value to say, not only to those who are, by birth, children of Africa, but also to those whose birth has caused them to be part of another cultural and religious background.

Furthermore, it is my belief that, while religious phenomena have certain commonality factors, not only on the continent of Africa, but worldwide, it is also essential to place specific phenomena in the particular framework to which they belong. For this reason, from a vast number of possibilities, I chose to introduce only five religious systems and their respective cultural settings. I do not propose to have said anything especially novel in this work but rather have relied on the work of others, simply correlating and extracting those elements that seemed to me to be religious in nature. I have given credit to the various authors where apposite throughout the body of the text and, in addition, I have included a list of suggested books for further reading on the various religious traditions. My sincere thanks go to those researchers who have given us such fine ethnographical and anthropological accounts upon which to draw, for example: Dorothea Bleek and Megan Biesele, Harriet Ngubane and David Hammond-Tooke, Marthinus Daneel, Colin Turnbull and others.

I trust that this book may serve the purpose of helping those of us who live on this beautiful continent to understand and appreciate one another more.

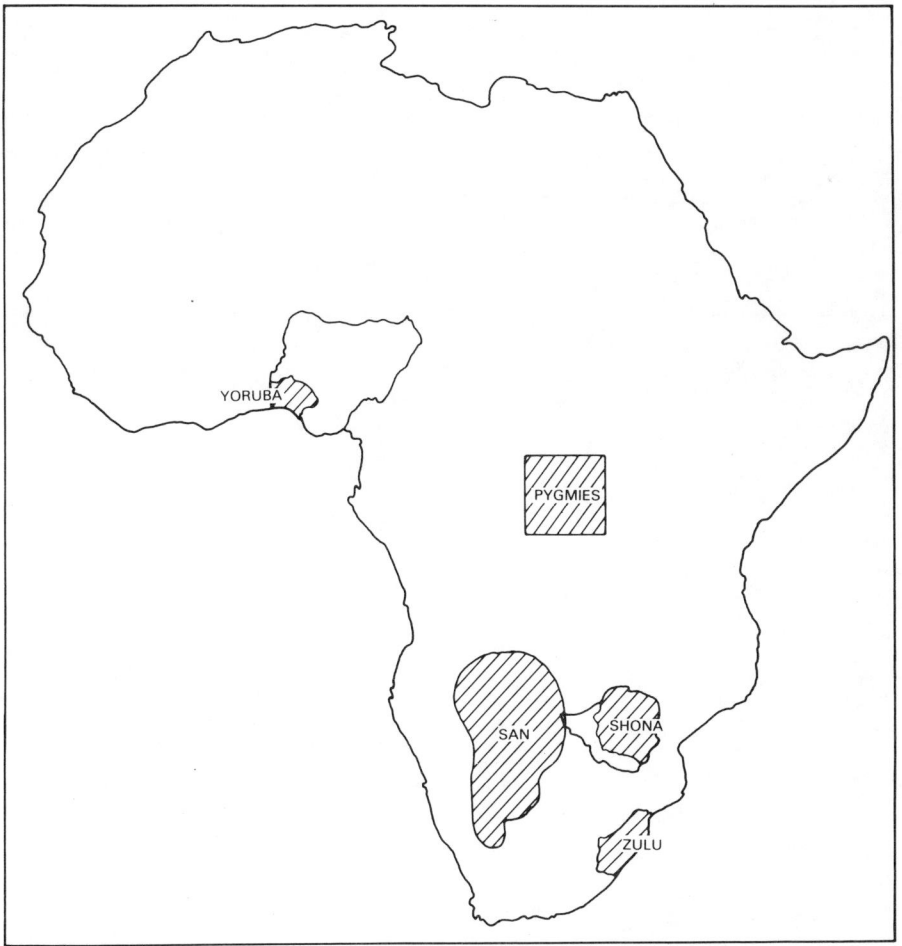

Figure 1 Map indicating approximate location of the cultures referred to in this book

CHAPTER 1

Introduction

> Closely interwoven with African culture, African traditional religion is a valid religious orientation worthy of consideration by people living in societies with other religious orientations.

Africa is not only one of the largest continents on planet earth, it may well prove to have been home to the very first human beings. Its size and history demand attention and respect. Since religion and culture are, in many ways, two sides of the same coin, those who seek to know about the people of Africa would do well to begin their inquiry with a review of the religious aspect of traditional African life. That, as can be gathered from the title, is where the focus of this book falls. At the outset, however, several things need to be said about African religion.

African traditional religions belong to a category of religious approaches worldwide which may be described as *primal religions*. These religions are often grouped together because they have come into existence independently in relatively isolated areas of the world and have no immediately apparent historical relationship to one another, nor to the major world religions such as Christianity, Islam, Hinduism or Buddhism.

Primal religions in general have no sacred written scriptures but are passed from generation to generation orally. They have no specific founder, although many of them do have tribal founders or heroes who are commemorated in sacred historical myths. Since they have no written creeds or dogmas, one cannot speak of either orthodoxy or heresy in their regard.

In primal cultures religion is a way of life. It is co-extensive with being human. As a result people in primal cultures do not engage in missionary activity. They do not attempt to convert people from other tribes or villages to their own religious ways of thinking or acting.

For much the same reason tolerance and flexibility are hallmarks of primal religions. It follows that even though people do not make an overt attempt to convert others to their ways of thinking and acting, there is a great deal of spontaneous borrowing and exchange of ideas. When people from differing religious cultures come into contact with one another, for example, it may be supposed that a troubled member of the one culture may imitate a ritual performed in a like situation by a person from another culture, especially if the initial outcome was successful. It is on the basis of this concept of a borrowing and exchange of ideas that attempts have been made to trace the historical development of certain African groups, especially among the Bantu-speaking peoples.

Because religion is such an integral part of life in primal cultures, early Western explorers and missionaries often failed to recognise it as such. In their reports and accounts some expressed the belief that the people with whom they came into contact had no religion. It is because of this misconception that the terms 'pagan' and 'heathen' came to be applied to these people. Obviously it is totally inappropriate to use such terms to refer to people in primal cultures, even though their religious orientations are not expressed by means of congregational-type worship, elaborate temples or rationalised creeds of faith.

In a similar way the term 'primitive' has come to have pejorative or patronising connotations. It is often taken to imply either backwardness, crudeness and stupidity, or otherwise a carefree life in a fictitious world of utopian bliss. Neither extreme adequately describes those peoples whose ancestors have resided for thousands of years in isolated areas of the globe. The term 'primal', if still not entirely apposite, is perhaps closer to the point, since it refers to that which is primary, first or basic. The use of this term enables scholars to categorise these peoples for purposes of consideration and discussion.

One must never lose sight of the fact, however, that there are great differences among primal peoples worldwide. This book does not attempt to deal with all of these, but rather focuses upon primal religion as it exists in Africa. Even here the differences are many and profound. A comprehensive survey of all the religions of Africa is beyond the scope of any single volume. Instead five groups have been chosen to represent the various primal religious orientations to be found on the continent.

Primal religions in Africa are commonly referred to as 'traditional religions' and this designation has been retained for the title of this book. It seems to describe more accurately the religious systems of the northern part of the continent than the word 'primal'. Once again, however, the word 'traditional' is not entirely suitable and certain remarks are needed to clarify its usage.

In this context the word 'traditional' is used to distinguish the religious orientation of African peoples from other world religions which are also to be found on the continent. Use of the word 'traditional' should in no way be taken to imply that these religions are, or ever were, static. Not only can the religious orientations of African peoples be seen to have been affected by both Islam and Christianity, but also it seems entirely unreasonable to assume that they were static prior to the arrival of these religions on the continent. Rather, it seems safe to conclude that, like religious alignments throughout the world, African religions were shaped both by outside historical forces, such as interaction with others due to migrations and warfare, and by internal religious pressure from such people as prophets or healers who were thinkers and leaders in their communities.

Since traditional religions are oral and their concepts passed from generation to generation by word of mouth, we do not have written records by which we can trace historical developments within a given group. Deductions in this regard must be made from relatively recent findings. Among other things the way in which African traditional religion has adapted itself to changing circumstances throughout the continent suggests that changes likewise occurred in the past.

The term, 'African religion' without any additional qualification, is likewise misleading. Both Christianity and Islam have co-existed with traditional religions on the continent of Africa for over 1 300 years. Christianity was established in Egypt and Ethiopia at a very early date, as was Islam over the whole of North Africa (Parrinder 1968:99). It must also be recognised that many changes have occurred within the last two centuries as far as religion on the continent is concerned. Not only have Islam and Christianity had a considerable influence on Africa, but they, in their turn, have been affected by African world views, so that today we can speak of an African Christianity or an African Islamic approach. Many groups have arisen which combine elements of traditional religion with either Islam or Christianity. Those new religious movements which combine Christianity with African religion are often referred to as 'Indigenous' or 'Independent' churches. Consequently if the term 'African religions' is used, it must include all these movements, as well as Hinduism and other religions in certain parts of the continent.

The term 'African traditional religion', often abbreviated to the initial letters ATR, can be used in either the singular or the plural. Reference has already been made to the great diversity which exists among religious approaches across the broad expanse of the African continent. The plural form is used for the title of this book to call attention to this diversity, emphasising thereby the great variety of concepts and practices which distinguish the religious systems of various language or cultural groups from one another. It is necessary to assert that there are many different African traditional religions.

On the other hand, it must also be acknowledged that according to some scholars there are a sufficient number of uniform characteristics distinguishing the religions of Africa from other primal or world religions, so that it is not entirely inappropriate to use the term in its singular form. It should be remembered, however, that there is no such thing as just *one* African religion and even the imposition of a unitary framework on all ATRs is highly problematical. Often scholars who consider African traditional religion in this way do so by giving attention to one or more religious orientations implying that these are representative of the entire continent. Such an approach can be misleading and is not the one adopted for this book.

Nevertheless there is justification for calling attention to some of the features which many ATRs seem to have in common, such as belief in a Supreme Creator, belief in spirit mediators, and recognition of evil as that which disrupts and disturbs both social and personal harmony and well-being. Various means are activated to keep these disruptive forces at bay, primarily the aid of men or women who are called and trained to deal with adverse spiritual forces. These people are the traditional doctors.

As you read the following chapters you will note that even these basic features are modified from one group to another and some of them, such as belief in spirit mediators, for example, or a precise concept of evil, seem to be absent especially among both the Mbuti and the San. Even belief in a transcendent creator prior to the influence of Christian missionaries among the Zulu and Shona has been called into question by some scholars.

In summary, then, it is correct to say that both unity and diversity are descriptive of the approach to religion found on the African continent. Furthermore, African religion is not static; in spite of opinions often expressed to the contrary, it is dynamic - growing and developing. The many new religious movements which have arisen in Africa are strong evidence of this fact.

It has been suggested by some people that the African world view cannot be called a religion as such. This, of course, depends upon one's definition of religion. If that definition focuses upon creeds, dogmas, organisations, a hierarchial priesthood or communal worship in elaborate temples, then of course ATR does not fit the description. But if one's definition of religion focuses on a spiritual quality which enables people to orient and live their lives, then ATR indeed qualifies.

Of course a definition of religion must include more than just the positive orientations which define life's goals and aspirations. It must acknowledge and make some attempt to deal with that which is negative, disruptive and undesirable as well.

Taylor (1963: 35-40) suggests that African people are inclined to objectify attitudes and feelings such as jealousy, hatred and fear so that what happens inside a person spills out to touch not only other people, but even the environment as well. Thus negative, selfish attitudes may take on a life of their own, as it were, and be conceptualised as witches and sorcerers. The corollary, of course, is that what happens outside a person (warfare, floods, land-grabbing) can likewise move into the very heart and core of an individual. People are closely bound to one another and to their environment so that a basic religious principle for ATRs is one which fosters harmony and well-being.

Therefore any statement which attempts to define ATR should include at least two dimensions - the horizontal and the vertical. ATR is, on the one hand, very much a part of the society in which it is found. It is thus oriented to this world and has a clear horizontal dimension. But that is not the entire story. ATR is also permeated by an awareness of the spiritual, invisible dimension of life. Trees, rivers, streams, rain are more than merely things to be utilised. They have a spiritual quality which unites them to human beings in a greater cosmic whole. The ancestors or living-dead continue to be a spiritual part of this greater cosmos even after they have ceased to exist as a physical part. The creator, and even creation itself, belong to this vertical or spiritual dimension of ATR.

Religion, then, is a means whereby people orient their lives concerning those areas beyond their control. It is recognition of and a reaching out toward awareness of a greater whole than oneself. These nebulous realities become concretised in structures and concepts enabling both good and evil to be explained and at least partially understood. These explanations, in turn, lead to an ethical stance and resultant actions towards other people and their surroundings. Religion, in fact, pertains to beliefs and practices which arise from events and experiences of a mystical nature. According to such a definition ATR can be viewed as a valid religion.

It is the contention of this book that a study of ATR is well worth the time and effort involved. For many people the study of religions in general is an appealing prospect. Others simply find the accumulation of data interesting. Yet others are curious about the continent of Africa and the people who inhabit it. One of the most accessible doors to an understanding of any culture is the religious orientation of its people. But there is a still more pressing reason for a review of African religions. This is to be found in the ontological nature of religion as it exists on the continent of Africa.

Modern people are faced daily with stressful, often frightening conflict situations which are continually changing. A review of ATR could conceivably remind us of our origins, of the very nature of our humanity. To study and share in African peoples' faith response, both to the numinous and to the physical world, is to enhance one's ability to perceive the spiritual quality in one's own physical environment. This is not to say that a person's own religious faith should be abandoned in favour of a 'return to nature' but rather that one's own orientation is often in need of revitalising. This can frequently come about by exposure to another's religion.

Increasingly in recent years scholarship seems to indicate that Africa may be the cradle of humanity, of *homo sapiens* (Twesigye 1987:83). If this claim is valid the study of religion as it has existed in many forms in Africa for hundreds of centuries takes on even greater significance. ATR is the context from which African philosophy, anthropology, soteriology and ethics have sprung. In fact, the entire African world view, which is often expressed in forms of art and dance, is rooted and grounded in an African religious approach to life.

Some years ago certain people with an empirically-oriented point of view jestingly referred to the African's (and other primal people's) reverence for both animate and inanimate objects, the implied accusation being that they were treated as if they had a life of their own. Unfortunately in the past the attitude of the Western world to nature was often one of exploitation for the supposed benefit of humankind. Africans were considered backward because they observed such things as totemic regulations or regarded their land as sacred to their ancestors. Recent years, however, have witnessed a striking change in this attitude on the part of Western people. Increasingly people of the world are coming to realise that our existence is not unrelated to the animals, plants, trees or even rocks and mineral substances which are found not only in our immediate environs, but in the most remote places of the earth. Perhaps African sacralisation of nature was, after all, a more accurate image of reality than was initially acknowledged.

It would seem, then, that it is of utmost importance to us, living in the dying days of the twentieth century, to look long and carefully at ATR to see if we can find seeds of renewal buried in that past heritage. Those of us who live on the African continent are best placed to conduct this type of investigation. Although this book is not intended to present ATRs as a paradigm for religious orientation, it is nevertheless hoped that it will inspire some of its readers to take a more serious look at some of the positive aspects of ATRs in order to enrich their own perspective.

Only five religious orientations, from many possibilities, have been chosen for review in the following pages. The story begins in southern Africa with the San people, who can seemingly lay claim to one of the longest histories of existence on this continent. It then moves eastward, still in the southernmost part of Africa to introduce the religious world view of the Zulu people. Chapter four enables the reader to travel northwards to consider Shona religion. Both Zulu and Shona religious orientations give some idea of the Bantu religious perspective. Chapter five reviews the religious orientation of the Mbuti pygmies who live in the Ituri Rain Forest region of Zaire. Finally the historical presentation of African religion is concluded with a review of Yoruba religion among the Negroid people of Nigeria. These five groups of African peoples were chosen to introduce the reader to the variety which exists in religious orientations throughout the continent. Both the Mbuti and San have a considerably different outlook religiously from the Yoruba people in the northwest, from the Zulu in the southeast or from the Shona in the central part of the continent. Likewise, differences can be seen to exist between the San and the Mbuti, as between the Zulu, Shona and Yoruba. Although none of these groups can be said to identify a uniform religious perspective, they are presented as independent systems more or less representative of their respective categories in order to provide a basis for initiating comparisons.

Very often ATR is discussed from a thematic or phenomenological perspective, whereby various phenomena or themes are explored and illustrated by reference to their presence in particular African religions. While under certain circumstances this may be an acceptable approach to the study of ATR, it can also lead to the misconception that all African religions fit into a single, unitary framework. The approach of this book is rather that the various phenomena are best understood when they can be comprehended according to their relationship and interconnectedness with one another. It is for this reason that a historical (in the sense of a story, not chronology) approach has been adopted. Chapter seven, however, attempts to extract some of the more salient features of ATR and present them in a thematic manner. In the final chapter an attempt is made to appraise the merit of African Traditional Religion/s with a view to the future.

This book has been written with the hope that it will be both interesting and beneficial, enabling its readers to discover hidden truths about their own beliefs as they read about those truths that have been discovered by others.

SUGGESTED READING

Ray, B C 1976. *African religions: symbols, ritual and community.* Englewood Cliffs: Prentice-Hall.

Mbiti, J 1975. *Introduction to African Religion.* London: Heinemann.

King, N Q 1970. *Religions of Africa.* London: Harper and Row.

CHAPTER 2

The elusive San

In this chapter the religious way of life of the Bushmen is described with reference to some of their myths, their concepts of God, the role of dance and trance in maintaining the health of individuals and groups, and the relationship between religion, the social unit and the environment.

HISTORICAL AND CULTURAL REVIEW

Early Portuguese, Dutch and English voyagers described a people occupying the coastal regions and later the central plateau of southern Africa. Who were they? Where have they gone? Polychrome paintings of animals, insects and people are found on rock surfaces inside caves in southern Africa. How and when were they thus inscribed? Who were the skilled artists? How did they ply their craft? Human footprints in the sand - who made them? Honey missing from a tree - who took it? A poisoned arrow flies swiftly to meet its mark - who shot it? The people who may provide the answers to these questions are the San - or Bushmen, as they are more commonly known - of southern Africa, and it is they who claim our attention in this chapter.

Viewed from one perspective, San religion is not truly representative of African religion overall; yet from another perspective it is the most African of all religions. Remnants of possible Bushman civilisations have been found dating as far back as 10 000 to 25 000 years. This long history in the land has naturally left its mark on almost the whole of southern Africa. The influence, as subtle as the San are elusive, can be detected in certain clicking sounds in words, especially among the Nguni-speaking people, as well as in various concepts pertaining to religion and culture.

This chapter attempts to answer the question, 'Who are the San?', by discussing their past and present habitats, as well as their linguistic, physical and cultural characteristics. With this as background, their religious orientation to life can then be brought into focus.

The best place to begin any story is at the beginning, so the first question we shall attempt to answer is, 'What are the origins of the San?' But even this initial query brings us face to face with that elusiveness which is so characteristic of the San. There are, however, some things which can be said about their origins. In all likelihood they were the earliest human beings to inhabit southern Africa. They are believed to be direct descendants of Late Stone Age people who somehow eluded that mainstream of civilisation which led to the cultivation of plants and the herding of animals. Thus the San, having inhabited southern Africa for more than 10 000 years, have survived until modern times as hunters and gatherers of food. They are entirely dependent upon their environment, which they not only utilise expertly, but to which they have learned to adapt their own unique life style.

Much of what we know about the San's past history is conjecture based on archaeological evidence, as is the case with all material from prehistoric times. Since the recorded history of southern Africa begins with the account of Vasco da Gama's voyage in 1497 and is followed, only after that date, by more prolific written accounts by Dutch and English explorers in the seventeenth and eighteenth centuries, our knowledge is very limited. We must attempt to reconstruct theoretically what the area was like before white settlers caused extreme disruption for the San and others, beginning at the Cape of Good Hope. Part of this conjecture is based on observation of the present-day San. While we must remember that human beings of 10 000 to 25 000 years ago may not have lived exactly like contemporary San hunters and gatherers do, we can hope to learn at least something from a careful comparison of the common elements found among the various groups of survivors still left today.

When the early explorers arrived at the southern tip of Africa their written accounts of the area and its inhabitants seemed to indicate three major groups of people. Only much later were these three groups clearly identified and named (at a symposium of the South African Institute for Medical Research in 1971). Early writers had described a yellow-skinned people they first met at the Cape who spoke a language characterised by strange clicking sounds and who were herders of cattle. Later these people came to be called Hottentots. Another people, similar in appearance although smaller in stature, were much more elusive and did not seem to adapt themselves to the Hottentots' pastoral way of life, often disappearing into the surrounding wilderness. They were called *Bosjesmans* (Bushmen) by the Dutch and Sanqua (San) by the Hottentots, who referred to themselves as the Khoikhoi. Still later another group, then inhabiting the inland areas farther north and the coastal areas to the east, was identified. Physically they were taller in stature and darker in skin colour. These were the Bantu or people.

While the cultural, physical and linguistic differences between these three groups need recognition - and, at times, even overemphasis for purposes of analysis and study - one should never lose sight of the extensive overlapping in these areas. The San and the Khoikhoi are the most closely related and are often considered collectively as the Khoisan peoples. All three groups must be viewed as African Negroid, although the Khoisan have a long history of differentiation from other Negroid strains (Tobias 1976:10). It has been suggested that the differences may have accelerated when the Bantu-speakers living farther north became agriculturlists and the Khoisan remained hunter-gatherers (Lewis-Williams & Dowson 1989:9).

In this chapter the three groups are referred to as: the San, who speak a variety of Bushman languages and whose economy was based on hunting animals and gathering natural foods; the Khoikhoi, who spoke a Hottentot language and were herders, primarily of cattle; and the southern African Negroes, who speak a variety of Bantu languages and were both herders and cultivators of food.

Most true Bushmen today live mainly in the Kalahari. But this is only the tail-end of their story. In prehistoric times, San peoples were spread, probably in small family or tribal groups, over most of southern Africa. When the first Dutch settlers arrived at the Cape, the San must have occupied a large part of the territories now known as the Republic of South Africa, Namibia, Botswana, Lesotho and Swaziland, as well as parts of Mozambique, Zimbabwe, Zambia and Angola.

Early historians reported the presence in Mozambique of small click-speaking people whom they called the Wak-wak, and archaeological remains of skeletal forms resembling the San have been found even outside southern Africa. This suggests that hunters and gatherers similar in appearance to the present-day San may have lived in Central and East Africa, and possibly right across the north-south extent of the eastern half of the continent (Tobias 1976:20). Gradually, however, these people were squeezed out of most of these areas by both Negroid and Caucasian peoples. Today they number somewhat less than 60 000, living largely in the semi-desert area of the Kalahari.

It is difficult to identify, and thus to number, the San population accurately. Both cultural adaptation and intermarriage have made it difficult to do so. Few today are still 'pure' hunters and gatherers, and of the total number of people classified as San, less than one-third still follow the classical Bushman life style outlined in this chapter. The remainder have adapted in varying degrees to Western cultural ways.

Some of the distinctive physical characteristics of the San have already been noted. They are somewhat smaller in stature than other southern Negroid people and their skins are lighter, varying in colour from light to medium yellowish brown.

In addition, the San also have relatively little hair on the face and body; their lips are of moderate thickness, even thinnish and inverted; the upper eyelids have a fold; they have transversely placed nostrils and small, somewhat flat faces; and the brain case is fairly large in relation to the face (Tobias 1976:21). Their hands and feet are generally smaller than those of other adults. Their skin, which is dry and soft, tends to wrinkle excessively as old age approaches. Their hair, fine and tightly curled close to their scalps, has the appearance of peppercorn tufts. They have wide cheek bones with almond-shaped, widely spaced eyes. Some of the women have a tendency towards steatopygia (a concentration of fat in the buttocks) and/or steatomeria (a concentration of fat on the thighs), although this characteristic does not seem to be as prominent as it possibly was formerly (SA Museum 1976:2). Certainly it should be remembered that these characteristics only obtain generally. As is true of people everywhere, there is great individual variation.

Numerous explanations have been offered for the characteristic physical appearance of the San. Most have proved to be either false or less than satisfactory. One of the better substantiated theories is that many of the anatomical traits characteristic of the adult San resemble those of all human infants but in the case of the San they have continued into adulthood. This phenomenon is known as neoteny.

Another theory tries to attribute the physical structure of the Bushmen to adaptation to desert conditions in the Kalahari. This might have been a satisfactory explanation, were it not for the fact that ancient San skeletons from other, non-desert areas in Africa show similar characteristics. This theory therefore probably has to be rejected.

It has also been suggested that the San are not true Negroes but show a similarity to the Mongoloid people of East Asia. This theory, while interesting, remains totally unproven and is contrary to anthropological evidence (Singer 1976:119).

One thing is certain - the San peoples are sensitive, caring human beings who deserve to be treated with understanding rather than merely as objects of curiosity. They have been subjected to ignominious treatment in a variety of ways and it is high time that the outside world accords them the respect they deserve.

The language of the San is characterised by unusual clicking sounds. Khoikhoi words also contained many of these same clicks, and this unusual language characteristic has even influenced the speech of the Nguni peoples, especially the Xhosa. Since these clicking sounds have no conventional symbols to represent them the following have been devised:

/ =	a dental click similar to that used in expressing sympathy or mild reproof (e g n/um = spiritual power related to bodily strength).
≠ =	an alveolar click similar to the above, but formed slightly further back in the mouth.
! =	a palatal click which produces a hard, popping sound (e g !Kaggen = the creator).
// =	a lateral click, making a sound like that used to urge a horse forward (e g //Nao = a man's name).

The San can be divided linguistically into three main groups: a southern, a central and a northern group. These major groups can in turn be broken down into smaller units such as the Naron, the //Aikwe, the Mbarakwengo, the G/wi, the Hei//om, the !Kung and the Auen (Jones & De Beer 1988:367). These should be viewed not as socially organised tribes, but simply as linguistic or geographical groupings. The real social group is the extended family unit or band which usually comprises two or three related married couples, their children and older adult dependants.

The San do not have a collective name for themselves, but take the name of their individual linguistic group, such as the !Kung whose name simply means 'persons', the Hei//om or Heikum (tree-dwellers), the //Kau//en or Auen and the Naron (insignificant people) (Schapera 1930:31-35). Known among Bantu-speakers as the Abatwa, they often refer to themselves as 'the real people' (*zhu/twasi*) reflecting that universally human feeling for those who share one's own language and cultural background. In paintings they often depict themselves as being very tall and a common greeting among some, 'I saw your shadow looming from afar', may reflect a healthy acceptance of their diminutive stature.

As has been stated, the San are hunters and gatherers of food. For the males hunting is not only a means of acquiring food but a highly skilled profession carrying varying degrees of prestige and honour. Hunting equipment consists primarily of a short wooden bow and two-part arrows with poisoned tips which break off, remaining behind in the victim. Clubs and spears are used as well once the poison from an arrow has done its work. Rope snares are used to catch birds, while small burrowing animals are dug out with long, thin sticks fitted with a hook at one end.

Arrows are carefully made, often by older men who can no longer run long distances. They are treated with a poison made from the larvae or grub of the chrysomelid beetle. This poison attacks the nervous system of the animal when it enters the bloodstream, causing a general paralysis and eventually death. It is claimed that the poison is not lethal if taken orally and certainly it in no way affects the meat of the animal it has killed (Taylor 1984:77). The maker of the arrow is accorded due respect, along with the successful hunter, and may be given the honour of dividing the meat of the animal killed with his arrow.

Hunting requires many skills and abilities, including camouflage, feint, marksmanship and stamina to run long distances, both in tracking and in following a wounded animal. Bushmen generally hunt in small bands of three or more men and/or boys. The meat from game thus acquired forms about 25 percent of the San diet; the skins and bones of the animals killed are used for clothing, ornaments and culinary utensils.

Girls (above the age of seven) and women are responsible for the gathering of seeds, berries, roots, bulbs and fruit which form the mainstay of the diet when meat is not available. A digging stick is used to unearth bulbs and roots. Women are usually responsible for collecting firewood. Honey is considered a special delicacy and men take full responsibility for acquiring this commodity in what can be a demanding and dangerous venture.

Although the San are called nomadic, this is true only in a limited sense. Small family bands hold unspoken, but definitely acknowledged, territorial rights over given areas which may relate to the growth of tsamma melons and water holes. Tsamma melons are important in that the gourds are used as cooking and eating utensils, besides providing food, seasoning and liquid when water is scarce, as it seasonally is in the Kalahari. This precious commodity, water, is carried and often stored in strategic places in 'flasks' made from ostrich egg shells.

When the San are moving from one seasonal location to another, they sleep more or less in the open. The women choose a spot, often near a clump of trees, and simply scoop or hollow out sleeping places in the sand. They may also erect a sheltering screen of branches and bushes for each family. When they arrive at one of their seasonal locations, however, they construct rather more substantial shelters by planting small trees in a semicircle and then bending over and interweaving the tops to form a rounded roof. These dwellings are used mainly at night, when a fire is made in front of each shelter. They are also used for storage purposes when an excess of food has been gathered.

The communal fire is, in fact, the symbol of home for the San. When a band settles in a new area, the eldest male is responsible for lighting the first fire with fire sticks. Thereafter each family lights its own fire with brands taken from the original one. The men are expected to sit on the left side of the fire, facing away from the hut. The San sleep on their sides with one ear tuned to hear any unusual noises in their surroundings.

The scant clothing worn by the San is made from dressed skins. Men usually wear only a loin cloth, while the women's apparel consists of one or more small aprons in front and a skirt, which is longer at the back, draped over the top of the aprons. A woman also wears a cloak over one shoulder, knotted on the right side. This is used to carry the food gathered each day, and serves as a pouch in which to carry her small children.

Leather sandals are often worn, and ornaments made from ostrich egg shells are greatly prized. They may be worn on arms, legs, forehead or neck. The San may trade or barter with non-Bushmen people but among themselves an exchange of gifts is the accepted custom (SA Museum 1976:26). This practice of sharing and having a minimum of individual possessions not only cements social relations, but is also an insurance against possible future need.

Surely, they appear to argue, it is more blessed to give away than to accumulate a surfeit of goods. When an animal is killed, certain pieces are customarily given to designated individuals in the tribe, who, in turn, are expected to give from their portions to others. Thus such emotions as jealousy and anger are kept to a minimum.

Music, dancing, art and drama are all part of the San way of life. Dances usually take place at night, often spontaneously, although they may have ritualistic, designated functions. The men and boys dance while the women provide the rhythm by clapping and singing. Women may also join in the dancing if and when they so desire. Musical instruments are often played by the men. These consist of stringed instruments (a stick and the string of their hunting bow, a type of harp or a thumb piano) and rattles made from moth cocoons.

Bushman art is well-known, although modern San confine their art work mainly to the decoration of household utensils. Rock paintings were generally made in prehistoric times, although some have been dated as recently as the nineteenth century. Numerous scholars have devoted their lives to a study of San rock paintings. Two books which are particularly important in this regard are: Vinnicombe, P 1976: *People of the eland*, and Lewis-Williams, D and Dowson, T 1989: *Images of power*.

Bushmen love to smoke; smoking is a social occasion where the pipe is passed from one to the other. Music, dancing, smoking and story-telling, at which the San excel, are all practised at the end of the day while the family sits around its fire before retiring to sleep. Most of the stories are in the form of myth or religious folklore. From San art and story-telling we have learned much of what we know about their religious orientation to life.

THE RELIGIOUS ORIENTATION OF THE SAN

As is true of all primal people, for the San religion and life are so closely interwoven that it is difficult to discuss the one without an understanding of the other. For this reason we have dealt first, and at some length, with the everyday life of the San. Now we shall look at some of the religious concepts which seem to emerge from their particular perspective on life.

Mythology

'When the earth was young, animals were people and the sun was small.' These words introduce the delightful atmosphere which pervades San mythology - small people contemplating a youthful world scaled down to their size, inhabited by animals, insects and birds. There are numerous ways in which San mythology differs from Bantu mythology. For one thing, San myths indicate that 'in the beginning' animals were people rather than the other way round. The notion that people originally were animals is a far more common theme in primal mythologies generally (Woodhouse 1984:4). In a Naron myth dealing with the acquisition of food, Dorothea Bleek (1928:49) records the closing words in her translated version as:

> At that time they both were men, the Ostrich was a man, the Paauw was a man. Two they were. Like this it was. All things were men. It was the beginning.

No discussion of San mythology can be undertaken without recognising the great variety and multiplicity of myths available for comparison and analysis. It must be remembered that the San live in small family units rather than in large tribes. These family units have been scattered over a wide area in Africa, hence many myths and many versions of each myth have arisen. Furthermore, among the Bushmen no one person's story or perception of the supernatural is regarded as being inferior to another's. Each time a story is told, with individual nuances and details added or subtracted, some new truth or aspect of divinity is brought to light. For example, stories of the /Xam San of the Cape, recorded over a hundred years ago by W H I Bleek and his sister-in-law, Lucy Lloyd, show both similarities to and differences from stories collected among the !Kung San, who are still living in the Kalahari today, and among other San groups such as the !Xo or the /Gwi living in more remote, northerly areas. Perhaps for the San there is no single, ultimate truth which is normative but rather multiple aspects of the truth which must be adhered to.

The Cape Bushman stories collected by W H I Bleek and L Lloyd revolve around a divine trickster figure who is involved in various acts of creation. His name, !Kaggen, has been translated as 'Mantis', although this translation is not entirely acceptable. A mantis is only one representation of !Kaggen who can also turn into a bull eland, a hare, a louse, a snake or a vulture. When not in an animal form he lives the life of an ordinary Bushman (Lewis-Williams & Dowson 1989:13). !Kaggen is very human in his handling of situations and characters, sometimes winning, sometimes losing life's battles. His wife, Kauru, is a dassie - a very human, docile one. They have three children - a daughter and two sons - as well as a beloved adopted daughter, Porcupine (!Xo) who, together with her family, figures more prominently in the Mantis stories than do the natural children. Porcupine, the natural daughter of the All-Devourer with whom she cannot live, is married to /Kwammanga, an aspect of the rainbow who has a contemplative, serious personality. Their two children - young /Kwammanga, who takes after his father, and talkative Ichneumon - often chide or give advice and guidance to their grandfather !Kaggen (suggesting perhaps the value of the cumulative ongoing nature of knowledge, as they may symbolise !Kaggen's future self - Van der Post & Taylor 1984:168). In addition !Kaggen has two sisters, Blue Crane and another who is the mother of his pet springbok.

Here is a revised version of one of the Mantis stories told by Bleek and Lloyd. The aetiological function of this myth is to explain the unique relationship which obtains between the Bushmen and the Eland. However, it also reveals the human dilemma of the people: they see the animals as close kin and yet, in order to survive, they must kill them. What is more, they love the taste of the meat they eat. This story, together with others, acts as a palliative, helping the people to resolve the paradox of their human condition. (Is this so very different from our modern dilemma - for example, the way we enjoy the use of manufactured products while at the same time abhorring the resulting pollution of our environment?)

The Mantis and the Eland

The Mantis made an Eland from his son-in-law /Kwammanga's shoe. /Kwammanga missed his shoe but neither he nor his wife had any idea what had happened to it. Meanwhile Mantis collected honey and fed it to the Eland which he had made as it came out of the reeds to eat. Mantis's family wondered why he brought so little honey home for them, and finally they sent Ichneumon to hide beneath a kaross and see what happened to the honey. Watching, he saw the Eland come from the reeds and drink the water into which Mantis had put the honey. Mantis even smoothed the honey-water onto the Eland's skin. Then Ichneumon jumped out from underneath the kaross. Quickly Mantis drove the Eland away, but Ichneumon confronted him with what he had seen. As they argued, Mantis denied the existence of the Eland. On his return Ichneumon reported what he had seen.

Secretly Porcupine's family plotted together and went to the pool where Ichneumon had seen Mantis feed and stroke the Eland. /Kwammanga then put honey into the water and called the Eland by name, whereupon it came out of the reeds to drink. As it drank /Kwammanga shot it. It ran back into the reeds, where it lay down to die.

Meanwhile Mantis was looking for honey to feed his beloved Eland, but he could not find any. Feeling a strange sense of foreboding, he went to the water to call the Eland, but it did not come. He wept as he sought his Eland, following its spoor and then the drops of its blood. At last he saw it lying dead in the reeds. Weeping and angry, he returned home. In the meantime /Kwammanga had commissioned meerkats to cut up the dead Eland. Mantis ran back to where the Eland lay. When he saw the meerkats busy slaughtering his animal, he tried to stop them by shooting arrows, which, however, missed their mark. Next he attacked them with a knobkerrie, but all to no avail. Finally a meerkat snatched the knobkerrie from Mantis's hand and, after beating him, made him collect wood for a fire. While he was thus busy, Mantis saw the Eland's gall bladder hanging on a tree. He pricked it open so that everything and everyone was covered in darkness. When he realised what he had done, he quickly removed his own shoe, which had red dust still clinging to it, and threw it into the sky where it became the moon. Later he explained to his grandson Ichneumon:

> The sun was shining brightly when I grew angry, because the Mierkat had wrestled with me and beaten me with a stick. I gathered wood, but I was angry. I made a hole for the fire, but I was angry. I put wood on the fire, but I was angry. I placed stones on the wood, I gathered more wood and put it on, I lighted the fire, but I was angry. The place was light because it was midday, but I was angry, so I pricked open the Eland's gall, because I wanted the sun to go into the dark. Then the sun set behind the mountain; darkness covered the earth. Darkness covered us all, even the Mierkats; we were all in the dark. Then I quickly thought about it, I quickly snatched off a shoe and spoke to it as I threw it up. I said: I am the Mantis, and this my shoe shall verily become the moon which shines in the dark.
>
> That is why the moon shines at night. That is why the moon is cold, because it is a shoe, it is leather. It is red because it has earth on it, the dust in which the Mantis had walked. The sun [sic] feels warm, because it is the sun's armpit. Under the sun people drink, for they feel thirsty, so they drink. Under the moon they make a fire, they also sleep, because the moon shines at night, it walks across the sky by night. When the sun feels warm people shoot springbok, they hunt springbok. All the ground is light, all places are light, all the people hunt.
>
> (Bleek 1923:5)

Among other things, this myth may be interpreted as revealing the bipolar phenomena of night/day, sun/moon complexes. Other myths seem to indicate an awareness of other bipolar conjunctions such as male/female, nature/culture, physical world/spiritual world, and the like.

An interesting and moving interpretation of this myth, albeit it from a Christian, Jungian, and possibly romanticised perspective, is given by Laurens Van der Post (1984:167-169). He sees the dilemma faced by Mantis as primarily that of a loving, caring creator. In creating the Eland from an old shoe (which some stories relate as having been thrown away by /Kwammanga), Mantis demonstrates that that which is despised by human standards is ultimately the stuff of new creation. Perhaps it is thus that the human spirit itself is renewed by the despised and rejected. The honey with which Mantis nurtures the Eland may symbolise that wisdom which proceeds from love. The tenderness and satisfaction which went into the act of creation was thwarted by the jealous, misunderstanding of others, those closest to Mantis. They, in fact, represent his future selves, the ones he is becoming. Thus his sorrow, while primarily over the loss of the Eland, is also sorrow for the separation which ultimately exists between creator and creature - the human dilemma which attends even the joy of parenthood. This inescapable bitterness is symbolised by the gall which, when the bladder is pricked, envelops everything in the darkness of despair and hatred - a hatred which obscures the inner vision of the soul.

In another version, it is a feather and not Mantis's shoe which enables him to brush the darkness away. In this version, however, it is Mantis's own shoe, with the soil of his weary travels still clinging to it, that eventually turns the darkness to light. This may suggest the inner spirit of the human soul which rises above the felt bitterness of an experienced moment to shine again, lighting the way no longer for oneself alone, but also for others.

Although the myths of the Bushmen people are richly varied, one myth is easily recognisable among all groups in spite of many variations. This is the myth of the origin of death in which the moon, filled with compassion for humankind, sent the hare to tell people they need not die, but could know the same renewal that the moon itself repeatedly experienced. But the hare bungled the message - some versions say intentionally, others unintentionally, simply due to the evil of haste. He told the people instead, 'Unlike the moon, who in dying is renewed, you, in dying, will not be renewed.' Since the spoken word was irrevocable, the message could not be changed. In great anger the moon hit the foolish hare on the mouth, splitting his lip. That split remains to this day as a testimony to the frustrated desire of a deity to bless humankind with the assurance of the renewal of life.

Another myth which Van der Post (1984:166) recalls from his childhood concerns a Bushman hunter who saw, one day, the reflection of a great white bird in the water of a deep, blue pool from which he was drinking. When he looked for the bird that had caused the reflection, it was nowhere to be seen, but the vision was so compellingly beautiful that he gave up his life's occupation as a hunter to devote all his time to a seemingly vain quest for the bird. At the end of his life his search eventually took him to the foot of an unscalable mountain where the bird reportedly dwelt. In his utter exhaustion he could go no further and lay down to die. Convinced that his search, and thus his entire life, had been in vain, he heard a voice say, 'Look up!' As he did so a single white feather came floating down. In this, his last moment of earthly existence, he reached out his hand and grasped the feather. Clutching it to himself, he died content. The name of that beautiful, elusive white bird, the story-teller related, is the Bird of Truth.

Although these few stories are merely an introduction to the tantalising world of Bushman mythology, they may, like the Bird of Truth, send you, the reader, on a lifelong quest to learn more about these people and the uncanny insight into life's realities that is revealed in their stories.

The Bushman concept of God

Before we consider this topic it might be profitable to ponder whether or not we ourselves have a concept of god, and, if so, how we would describe god to a person unfamiliar with our respective religions. This, of course, is not an easy task. It is necessary, therefore, to acknowledge that our attempt to describe a Bushman's concept of god is inevitably inadequate and incomplete. In the first place, early, often untrained ethnographers (outsiders) questioned ordinary San people about the nature of their god. In addition, they listened to myths and observed ritualistic activities and then formulated opinions as to what the people believed. From these early accounts, others followed. Finally, an attempt was made to correlate and review these various opinions with due acknowledgment of the individualistic, multiple nature, not only of San myths, but of all their religious concepts. Perhaps we should call to mind the San myth of the Bird of Truth at this point.

Furthermore, it should be borne in mind that to the San, as to most primal peoples, the name of god is too charged with sacred power to be spoken lightly. Thus a variety of pseudonyms have been devised for referring to god. The !Kung, for example, have seven divine names and one human name for the great god. This raises the question as to whether the San recognise a single god (monotheism) or a multiplicity of gods (polytheism), although this is somewhat beside the point in that neither term is truly appropriate. Marshall (1962:237) gives detailed descriptions of anthropomorphically conceived divinities among the !Kung. She notes also that definite changes had occurred in the !Kung perceptions of divinity over a period of time. As far as she could determine these were not due to outside influences. Also a measure of dualism that seems to be present in the conceptual forms of the divinity should be noted, pointing perhaps to the fact that the perceived nature of god is clearly not easily defined.

The following summary of Bushman beliefs about divinity is largely an analysis of an account by Megan Biesele (1978:162-165).

In most groups there is belief in a greater and a lesser god, as well as in other supernatural beings. The greater god is regarded as a supreme, good creator, although he is often highly anthropomorphised. He can send both good and bad fortune to people; he created the elements necessary for human sustenance, taught the people the skills necessary for their survival, and gave them the knowledge and skill to cure themselves by dancing. He dwells in the eastern sky where the spirits of the dead also go and are rejuvenated.

It has been suggested that the trickster figure, Mantis, is a representation of the Bushman god. It may be best to consider him as representing only one aspect of god, possibly that of a caring creator.

The greater god sends misfortune either through the spirits of the dead or through the lesser god who lives in the western sky. This lesser god is more often equated with that which is treacherous and evil, although both gods have ambivalent characters, capable of both harmful and beneficial actions against the people. Neither is connected totally with sin or unethical conduct. Since 'sinful' actions are generally related to the community, they are dealt with there in a this-worldly manner. There is, however, one exception. If a person is maltreated by his family, which should protect him/her, god is on the side of the maltreated individual. He then punishes the group by taking the person to stay with him in his dwelling in the sky.

Both the greater and the lesser god may be approached by people in shamanic trance, and also at other times through informal prayer. Prayers to the moon by some Cape Bushmen have been recorded, but certainly these do not amount to moon worship. No doubt it is closer to the truth to say that in these instances the moon is personified in the same way that rain is among the same Cape Bushmen.

Rain is said to both 'thunder' and 'flash with lightning', or to carry people off in a whirlwind when angry because certain taboos or observances have not been kept. It is said that rain can also appear in the form of an animal, especially the eland. According to some, leading an eland across the countryside will cause rain to fall in times of drought. Some groups even differentiate between male and female rain, the former being violent and frightening while the latter is gentle and more desirable.

Two other concepts found among certain San groups deserve attention. They are represented by the words //gauwa and entlow or n/um. //Gauwa has been said to refer to the spirits of dead people, to malevolent messengers from the great or lesser god, and to 'the wind that howls'. Dorothea Bleek (1928:26) indicates that the Naron and the Auen seemingly equate //gauwa with ghosts or with people who have died, but she also adds, 'Some individuals seemed to believe in a supreme //gauwa ... who lives in the east near the Great God.' Jonas and De Beer (1988: 374) indicate that the !Kung use the word as the principal designation for the lesser god, while Marshall (1962:238) indicates that among the Nyae-Nyae !Kung the word has three interpretations. It may refer to the spirit of a dead person (the plural form //gauwasi is more common); it may be the name applied to children born to the gods (again //gauwasi), or it may be used as one of the seven names which the great and lesser gods have in common.

In addition there is a belief in a power (which might be similar to that represented by the term 'mana'), that is present in certain people at certain times in their lives - women in childbirth, newborn babies, menstruating women, young men at initiation, et cetera. Among some San groups, this power is called *entlow* and, among others, *n/um*. It is believed to have a great effect upon the weather - so important to people like the San who spend most of their time out of doors. According to Biesele (1975:6,7) n/um should not be considered as a physical substance but as a latent supernatural power activated in singing and dancing, by the rhythm produced by the gourd rattles of the men and the clapping of the women. It is the power which is present at a healing dance.

Once again the danger of attempting too rigid a categorisation of San beliefs about divinity must be stressed. Their concepts are mystical ones in which a supernatural presence is all-pervasive. In the final analysis, divinity is life - breathing, throbbing in all aspects of the universe.

Dance, trance and health

Nowhere is the dynamic character of the San world more pronounced than in their dancing. Although their dancing has a ritualistic, religious quality, it remains natural and spontaneous. Towards the end of the day a few children at play may begin a rhythmic game which captures the attention of some of the adults, who may join in the dancing. Gradually others are drawn in and soon the entire group is captivated by the spell of the now glowing firelight, the singing and rhythmical clapping of the women. Some of the men may begin to leap and dance around the fire as the children gradually retire to join their mothers who are now seated on the ground around the fire. Now and then some of the women may also join the male dancers, usually for relatively short spells.

The dancing may well continue until dawn begins to lighten the distant horizon. As it reaches a peak of excitement, one or two of the men or women may go into trance. They are now filled with the power of n/um - indeed the entire atmosphere is charged with it. These are the healers or medicine men. In fact, it is not inappropriate to call them shamans, as there are striking similarities between their beliefs and activities and those of classical Asian shamans.

Although trance is not unusual among the San, not all become accomplished healers. These may have been chosen at the time of their initiation for more intensive teaching (Bleek 1928:28). Among some groups only men are healers, while women have been known to be healers in other groups. It has been estimated that among the !Kung about one-half of all adult men achieve trance during their lifetime. While the dance is in progress, a sick person may be laid to one side and gradually the dancers form a circle around the patient. The men take part of their bodily strength in the form of perspiration from their armpits and press it over the sick person's body. The shaman then receives the foreign object causing the illness into his own body, either when the patient sneezes or by the action of sniffing or sucking. Finally the healer sneezes the pathogenic object out through his nostrils, thus causing his nose to bleed. Alternatively it is believed to be expelled through the shaman's upper back. The shaman may make animal-like noises during trance, as a result of the pain caused by these foreign, illness-causing objects. In trance he can also perform such miraculous feats as handling fire or burning coals. He is believed to have supernatural vision in this state, so that he is able to see into a person's body to locate the source of illness. He can see and even travel great distances outside his body and may climb 'the thread of the sky' to the place where god himself resides and where the spirits dance (Taylor 1984:94-94).

Sickness and evil are understood by some to be the result of small arrows sent by a bad or foreign shaman or by god or one of his messengers from among the spirits of the dead. The healing trance is not always effective and the shamans understand that they are doing battle with supernatural forces. In fact, among some groups they may leave the body of the sick person and the firelit circle of dancers. They run off alone into the dark, where they shriek and often hurl insults at the spirits of the dead or at the god who is causing the illness, insisting that he take back the evil he has sent and that he should not be so greedy as to want to take this sick person away from the group.

Sometimes the patient dies, but always the power of n/um which is intensified and released by the occasion restores the health and wholeness of the San unit. The singing, the fire, the dancing and the trance all work together to activate n/um, especially in and through the person of the shaman.

Religion and the community

The San community is always a small one. When the weather is harsh and game is scarce, the band breaks up into smaller single family units and waits until living conditions improve. Then the families reunite into a somewhat larger, more joyful band. Social activities always have religious significance, although the two are not synonymous in that religion has both a personal and a social aspect.

The nodal points of San life - times of change and crisis - are filled with an awareness of the power for good or ill which is inherent in them. Such an occasion is the birth of an infant. Already during her pregnancy the mother has been the object of certain taboos which she or others near her have observed. Now, when her time of labour draws near, she goes alone into the bush. She collects soft grass on which she herself may rest and later lay her newborn child. Although men are expressly excluded from this area of special female power, another woman or two may accompany the mother-to-be if it seems that their help will be necessary. Among some groups a female shaman may be called upon to assist if the situation warrants it. Usually, however, the mother gives birth alone and, although Bushmen love their children, there are no special ceremonies conducted in connection with the birth, nor later at the time of name-giving. Their joy, although subdued, is sustained.

In fact, practicality prevails even at birth, for if twins are born, or if children are born so close together that the mother cannot breast-feed both (mothers suckle their children up to the age of three or four), the newborn infant is not permitted to live. It is the obligation of the mother to quickly extinguish its life. Should she fail to do so and return with it to the community, it would then become a true person in which case it would no longer be ethical to extinguish life.

Girls and boys are equally welcome in the San family band. They begin to share in group responsibilities when they are about seven or eight years of age. Boys join the men in their hunting expeditions and girls help their mothers with the gathering of vegetable-type foods.

Marriage and initiation are closely linked. As might be expected, customs regarding these life crisis situations differ from group to group. Usually initiation for a boy is related to his hunting expertise. When he has learned to hunt and has made at least one successful kill, he is ready to consider marriage. In some groups he may be expected to go to an initiation school consisting of ten to twelve adolescent male youths. Women are excluded from the initiation areas, where the boys may be subjected to harsh treatment, including withholding of food and water.

According to Schapera (1930:126), ritual dancing is practised and the appearance of a supernatural being (Hishe for the Naron) indicates that this is an introduction into the mysteries of the tribal religion. Cicatrisation may be performed on both boys and girls, but circumcision is not generally practised except among the Hiechware of the Eastern Kalahari. Among the !Kung a boy is ritually scarified by his father after he has killed a large animal such as an antelope, a giraffe or a buffalo. He may be scarified twice, once on the right side for the first male animal and once on the left side for the first female animal. This rite is believed to strengthen his power as a hunter by giving him keen sight and accuracy in shooting arrows (Jonas & De Beer 1988:373).

The young men are now permitted to consider marriage to a girl with the consent of both sets of parents. This marriage, among some groups, may have been initiated at an earlier date by ritual capture which was, in all likelihood, prearranged (Bleek 1928:33). At this early stage marriage simply means that the young man joins the band of his in-laws and thereby adds his hunting skills to those of the other males in the group.

A man's first wife is usually very young. While the husband is from eighteen to twenty years of age, the girl may be only ten or eleven years old, or even younger. The marriage is not consummated until the girl has had her first menses and corresponding initiation ceremony. Only then are the young couple permitted to live together as man and wife.

A girl's initiation is performed individually as each one comes of age. She is taboo during her entire period of menstruation and is isolated in a specially built hut, where certain ritual actions are observed. Some of these seem to reflect a death-rebirth symbolism. Among some tribes a nightly Eland Bull dance is an important part of this initiation.

Among the !Kung the girl is carried to the initiation hut by a kinswoman other than her mother. Her head is covered and she is not permitted to touch the ground. While she is in the hut, designs are painted on her forehead and cheeks with red powder (Jonas & deBeer 1988:373).

At the end of the first menstruation and initiation, a young San girl is permitted to consummate her marriage. She now lives in a hut newly built by her mother, and she takes her place among the other women of the band. The young couple are expected to reside with the wife's family group until after the birth of one to three children. They are then free to join another band if they wish to do so. Usually this is the band of the husband's family where he may one day become the elder of his clan.

Among some groups monogamy is preferred although a second wife is not forbidden. Among the !Kung polygynous marriages are highly favoured. Separation and remarriage also occur (Bleek 1928:34).

Death for the San is treated with the same seemingly casual approach as birth. When a person dies he/she is buried with his/her possessions in a fetal position, knees bound by rope close to the chest. The body is laid on its left side, facing east, in a newly dug grave, close to the band's camp site. The grave is filled and covered and the family, after saying farewell to the loved one, moves on to a new location and avoids the burial spot for several years. There are no formal mourning rituals or ceremonies. When people become too old to accompany their family on a long, difficult march during times of drought, they may be placed in a sheltered spot with a supply of food and water and left behind. If an adequate supply of food and water is found within a relatively short distance, some of the family will return to fetch the abandoned old one, but if not, they simply avoid that place, knowing that death has come and hyenas have seized the remains (Bleek 1928:35).

Thus, like other primal people who must conserve every bit of energy so as to ensure the survival of the group, the San have no ethical objections to either infanticide or euthanasia if these become necessary. Death is accepted as the natural conclusion to every life on earth. While they are aware of the balance which must be maintained in nature, of which they are a part, they seemingly have a vision which transcends their mere earthly existence.

Religion and the environment

This transcendent vision is apparent in the San's attitude to their environment. All of nature is invested with a mystical, religious quality. People do not speak crudely or readily about their beliefs, but when these beliefs are expressed, it can be seen that they are filled with deep symbolic significance.

The stars, for example, are described as the watchful eyes of dead ancestors or as great hunters. The morning star is the greatest, since the night quickly disappears to make way for him.

The night sky is said to be filled, not only with the visible stars, but also with music and the noise of the hunt.

In addition to the eland, which is held in reverence, the steenbuck is said to exude a magic which so captivates and charms a hunter about to shoot it that he misses altogether. A mystical relationship exists between the ratel (or honey badger) and a little bird, the honey-diviner. The San are well aware of this relationship and treat both as fellow seekers after the much desired honey.

Some physical features of the environment are believed to be invested with supernatural power and are accorded due respect and awe. The Tsodilo Hills, for example, are a special sanctuary to the !Kung Bushmen who live in that part of the Kalahari and are sacralised accordingly in myths and taboos.

The religious aura which characterises the San's relationship to their environment is nowhere more apparent than in the Bushman paintings made on rocks and in caves many years ago. Their charm and mystical quality reach out and touch us who live in another age and another culture, so that we may well agree with Laurens Van der Post when he recollects: 'Love is the aboriginal tracker, the Bushman on the faded desert spoor of our lost selves' (Van der Post 1961:136).

The religious orientation of the San cannot be separated from their social and environmental orientation. The practical affairs of life such as hunting and gathering of food, rearing of children or moving camp are validated by mythical concepts and consequently all of life is embued with a mystical aura. Life is energy and energy is divine. Participation in life's activites both releases and renews that divine energy. Life's beginnings are thus united with life's endings in a continuing cycle which has endured throughout countless centuries. If, in fact, the San way of life is finally giving way before Western infiltration, something of great value may be about to be lost to the entire family of humankind. In this age when ultramodern technology is carrying us rapidly beyond all known horizons, let us hope that something from the Bushman way of life can be taken with us into the future.

SUGGESTED READING

Lewis-Williams, D & Dowson, T 1989. *Images of power*. Johannesburg: Southern Book Publishers.

Van der Post, L & Taylor, J 1984. *Testament to the Bushmen*. Middlesex: Viking.

Woodhouse, B 1984. *When animals were people*. Mellville: Van Rensburg.

Vinnicombe, P 1976. *People of the eland*. Pietermaritzburg: University of Natal.

CHAPTER 3

The Zulu people of Natal

In this chapter the religious orientation of the Zulu people is viewed in terms of two major streams: belief in the spiritual power of divinity, and belief in the power of the continuing community, both visible and invisible.

HISTORICAL REVIEW

The previous chapter dealt with the religious world view of the San who inhabit certain arid regions of southern Africa. In this chapter we remain within the same broad geographical area - South Africa - but the focus shifts towards the eastern coastline, to the province known as Natal, so named by the Portuguese explorer Vasco da Gama in 1497 as he sailed along the spectacularly beautiful but harbourless coast on Christmas Day (*o Dia do Natal* in his native Portuguese). The inhabitants of this area only became known to the European world much later, during the early 1800s. Prior to this a related group of Nguni-speaking people, the Xhosa, had come into contact with white Boer farmers as they migrated eastward, both inland and along the seaboard, from the foothold which they had secured at the Cape.

These Nguni-speaking people encountered by the white farmers differed in many respects from the Khoisan people with whom the newcomers to the African continent had had dealings up to then. Some of the differences were linguistic; others were physical, economic and social. To the white newcomers, however, one cardinal difference seemed to lie in the area of temperament. Whereas the Khoisan had either retreated from conflict situations or acquiescently become absorbed into Western culture, the newly encountered Bantu people resisted. According to some historians, these people represented the vanguard of a movement of African peoples gradually traversing the continent in a southerly direction. If so, this may partially account for their hostile resistance to displacement. Such an interpretation of history must not be misconstrued as support for the myth that the southern part of Africa was empty of people prior to the arrival of white settlers. Dark-skinned people have a very long history of habitation in the southern part of the continent.

Although some of the terms used above, such as Bantu and Nguni, partly defy definition, the following is a limited explanation. The word 'Bantu' comes from *abantu*, the plural of *umuntu*, which means 'person'. Bantu, then, simply means 'the people' - people of Africa south of the Sahara. The term was first used by Bleek as early as 1858 and was based upon the common occurrence of the stem *ntu* in many of the languages in southern Africa. Thus the distinction between Bantu and other peoples of Africa is based primarily on linguistic rather than racial grounds. It may be stated that, in general, people living in the north-western part of Africa, have a conglomeration of languages and dialects many of then unrelated to each other. Africans living in the central and southern part, however, have one Ur-Bantu language, evidence of which is to be found in every Bantu language and dialect. There are also certain physical and basic religious distinctions between those in the north-western and central-southern regions.

The Bantu language group, which is found in southern Africa, comprises nine major languages. Although these languages are related, there are definite variations among them. These have resulted in an even greater number of dialects, all, however, retaining certain grammatical similarities.

Linguistic criteria can be applied to differentiate further between the various Bantu peoples within the borders of South Africa, so that ethnographically the people have been classified as Nguni, Tsonga, Sotho and Venda. The Nguni-speakers may be subdivided into the Xhosa of the Cape whose language seemingly contains elements borrowed from the Khoisan people, the Zulu of Natal, the Swazi and the Ndebele of the Transvaal. As might be suspected, however, these classifications entail gross oversimplification. Not only is there much overlapping as well as inexplicable similarities and dissimilarities between the various groups; there are also small enclaves of people who do not seem to fit into any of these categories (Van Warmelo 1974:58).

In addition to linguistic criteria for purposes of differentiating between the various groups, other factors must also be taken into account - culture, economic systems, social structure, tribal or chiefdom limits, political and geographical boundaries. Unfortunately for those who seek to classify the people of South Africa, the application of these criteria does not always yield consistent categories.

Who, then, are the Zulu (Bantu, Nguni) people of Natal? Perhaps we should turn to history for the answer. In the late seventeenth or early eighteenth century a relatively small African clan migrated into northern Natal. From the name of their family chieftain, Zulu, son of Malandela, they became known as the people of Zulu (amaZulu) or, since 'Zulu' means 'the heavens', perhaps they thought of themselves as 'people of the heavens'.

The more recent history of the Zulu people, beginning with their leader Senzangakhona and his illustrious son Shaka, is relatively well-known. In Senzangakhona's day the Amazulu probably numbered no more than 1 500 people scattered over the rolling green hillsides of Natal. There were other Nguni-speaking tribes in the same general area; some were larger, such as the Mthethwa, and some smaller, such as the Elangeni. By the time Shaka was assassinated in 1828 after ruling for approximately twelve years, a new day had dawned for the Bantu people of southern Africa. Approximately two million people had been killed either in warfare or at Shaka's express command, but a few strong nations had emerged from what had previously been merely scattered tribes. Among those nations, the Zulu were the strongest, numbering a quarter of a million and inhabiting the coastal strip from the Swazi border on the Pongola River to central Natal, and from the coast inland as far as the Drakensberg range. This is roughly the territory known today as Zululand.

CULTURAL REVIEW

Although many present-day Zulu people have moved beyond the borders of Zululand and have, to a large degree, become urbanised, others have remained and still enjoy a traditional life style. There are many people of Zulu ancestry who work in South Africa in varying occupations - from university professors, leaders of industry and administrators to labourers and housewives. The focus of this chapter, however, falls upon those, both past and present, who have continued to follow the traditional life style. Political structures exist to unite urban and homeland Zulu. An example is the organisation known as Inkatha, led by Chief Mangosuthu Buthelezi, to whom approximately 1,5 million Zulus pledge their support. Modern Zulus are not only aware but proud of their cultural heritage and, like all of us, they perpetuate remnants of that heritage in their modern life style and world view.

Traditionally a Zulu person belongs to both a lineage and a territorial division. While these may coincide, they do not necessarily do so.

A territorial division, called a chiefdom, is governed by a chief (*inkosi*). While the chief's clan predominates in his own territory, other lineage clans may also be represented as a result of, for example, intermarriage. A chief's territory may be subdivided into smaller units called homesteads (*umuzi*), each under the immediate authority of an appointed headman whose position is not hereditary: should he fail to perform his duties adequately, he can be replaced. The Zulu chief is responsible to his own councillors and both past custom and mutual agreement are honoured in any form of decision-making. Each chief owes allegiance to the Zulu king (paramount chief) and collectively the chiefdoms form the Zulu nation (Ngubane 1977:13).

While a person can change his place of residence and thus his chiefdom, he cannot change his clan or lineage membership. That is his inheritance by birth.

The nuclear family, consisting of a man, his wife and their children, is as important among Zulu people as it is among most other people throughout the world. Traditional Zulu families live in homesteads or kraals consisting of one or more dwellings. Since a man may have more than one wife, each wife has her own hut and, together with her children, forms a distinct family unit. Each hut is divided into two sections, the right side for men and the left side for women. An area to the back of the hut, the *umsamo*, is reserved for offerings to the ancestors. This is their special place, as is the cattle kraal.

Unlike familial structures in many other cultures, however, the Zulu family is more intense at the local level and gradually broadens outwards to form a large social organisation which can be termed a clan. Technically a clan (or lineage) is composed of all those who bear a common praise name (*isibongo*) or surname. A clan often has an identifying song or anthem but is not totemic among the Zulu. For practical purposes, however, only those who live in a given general area and can trace their common paternal ancestry back for several generations are considered 'those we eat with' (at ritual gatherings) and among whom exogamic marriage regulations strictly apply.

This agnatic structure which is most intense at its local core is strengthened by various behavioural patterns, such as the names by which relatives refer to one another, the respect and reciprocation which are expected between certain members of a family and particularly by the custom of *hlonipha* for relatives-in-law. Hlonipha (literally to have shame or to shun through bashfulness) may be observed by means of particular actions or by refraining from using specific words in the presence of certain in-laws. A married woman, for example, is expected to keep her body covered from her armpits and shoulder-blade downwards in the presence of her father-in-law, all his brothers, the elder brothers of her husband, her mother-in-law and all other wives of her father-in-law. Likewise she must not use the name of any of these above-mentioned in-laws but must substitute another word instead. In fact she should not even use the name of her husband and must rather refer to him as the father of one of his children (Krige 1950:30).

At birth a Zulu child is strengthened with medicines and the umbilical cord must be buried secretly. There are other rites of passage as well, such as the piercing of a child's ears at about nine years of age and the incorporation of young men into regiments based on age group. An unusual feature is that the Zulu do not practise circumcision. Consequently young people do not attend circumcision schools, although this is common practice among most Bantu peoples. The onset of puberty, nevertheless, is marked by special individualised ceremonies.

Another outstanding characteristic of the Zulu people is their love of cattle. This is observable in a number of customs, one of which (according to early recorders) concerns the arrangement of their beehive-shaped dwellings into kraals. The cattle pen customarily occupied the central position in the kraal, with the huts arranged in a circular pattern around it. When a chief died, he was buried at the gate of his cattle byre. From early times the Zulu were able to enumerate and describe with great accuracy each animal in a herd that might number thousands. Cattle represent wealth but, more importantly, they provide a symbolic means, more binding than a Western treaty, of uniting families and tribes through the lobola marriage system. The connection which exists between the cattle and the ancestors of each tribe is also indicative of the deep, abiding symbolic value attached to each animal.

Obviously much more could be said by way of description and explanation in answer to our initial question, 'Who are the Zulu?' Since a major part of the understanding of any culture derives from insight into its religious orientation, we turn now to that aspect of Zulu life.

THE RELIGIOUS ORIENTATION OF THE ZULU PEOPLE

The Zulu life view is far more holistic than that of Western oriented societies where religion, work and home are often compartmentalised. The Zulu world is integral, with a supernatural dynamic power pervading all aspects. Therefore all human actions, personal as well as social, are responsible actions, imbued with religious significance. Both time and distance are perceived fully in terms of here and now. What is present gives substance and meaning to what is not. Any distinction between what is normally called religious beliefs and the social context of Zulu life is probably artificial. Nevertheless, for purposes of study, an attempt has been made to unravel the intricately interwoven strands of belief and action so as to present what seem to be the principal religious beliefs of the Zulu people.

Belief in a supreme sky god

One of the first observations of a religious nature made by early travellers, explorers and missionaries to Natal was the apparent acknowledgment by the Zulu of the existence of a Supreme Being, whom they appeared to consider responsible for creation. On the basis of both personal interviews with Zulu people and information gleaned from Fynn and others, Shooter (1857:159) writes:

> The Kafirs of Natal and the Zulu-country have preserved the tradition of a Being whom they call the Great-Great and the First Appearer or Exister. He is presented as having made all things - men, cattle, water, fire, the mountains, and whatever else is seen.

The name 'Great-Great' which Shooter uses is the translation of the Zulu word *uNkulunkulu*. This is the name the missionaries subsequently used to refer to god. Another name, *uMvelinqangi*, which Shooter translates as 'First Appearer or Exister', was, in fact, more correctly understood by the Zulu as referring to a supreme creator. It seems that the early missionaries preferred not to use this name due to its deep association with Zulu mythology concerning creation. The name uNkulunkulu could be thought of as expressing antiquity or age, possibly implying profound wisdom - the old, old one (as one might speak of a great-greatgrandparent), while the name uMvelinqangi may convey the notion of priority. Modern Zulu writers seem to show a preference for the name uMvelinqangi.

Other names which the early missionaries understood to refer to the Supreme Being were *uHlanga*, denoting an original source of being, and *iNkosi yezulu*, which means 'chief' or 'lord of the sky'. Numerous praise names are attributed to the lord-of-the- sky, such as *uMdali* and *uMenzi*, both of which imply that iNkosi is the source of all that is. The names *uMpande* and *uNsondo* give the idea that iNkosi is the one who causes growth in plants, not only originally, but continually. The names *uSomandla* and *uMninimandla* indicate that he is almighty and all powerful. *Amandla* which is the Zulu word for power is likewise related to wisdom and knowledge (Berglund 1976:35,36). From these names it might be inferred that iNkosi is understood to be an omnipotent, omniscient creator.

Numerous questions surround the Zulu people's precise conception of a Supreme Being before the arrival of the missionaries. Was he simply a 'first ancestor' - the first human, like Adam in Semitic religions? Did the various names all refer to the same Being, or did the Zulu believe in a creator god alongside other divinities who controlled the weather, the destiny of human beings and so forth? To what degree was the Supreme Being understood to be a creator god? If this being was in fact a creator, to what extent had it become a *deus otiosus*, withdrawn from any involvement in human affairs? Although it may not be possible to give final answers to these and similar questions, the names given to the Supreme Being seem to support the view that the Zulu already had an established belief in a Supreme Being prior to the arrival of the missionaries.

Although prayer is seldom addressed directly to this Supreme Being, it is not true to say that he or she is not worshipped at all. For example, on certain hills or mountains in Zululand there is a level place where it is possible for people to kneel in prayer. These mountains (*izigupo*) are held in reverence and prayer may be directed heavenward from these spots. They are resorted to particularly in times of drought, when rain is urgently requested, or by barren women desiring children.

Perhaps one reason why direct prayer to the lord-of-the-sky is not more common is the tremendous respect in which he is held. He is too great to be approached except through the proper channels - the ancestors. Thus a line of communication is drawn from the living Zulu mediators (elders of the clan or diviners) via the ancestors to the Supreme Being.

Zulu creation myths provide further insight into their comprehension of the Supreme Being. One of the best-known stories indicates that people came (or were broken off) from a bed of reeds, which metaphorically can mean 'source of being'. This has been interpreted to mean that the nations (or Nguni tribes) were broken off from an original 'source of being', whatever that may have been.

Another myth tells how a mischievous young man was punished by iNkosi by being sent to earth through a hole in the sky. After the hole had been opened in the floor of the sky, iNkosi tied an intestine or umbilical cord (*ithumbu/inkhaba*) around the young man's waist and lowered him to earth. The young man then cut himself loose from the cord connecting him to the sky by means of a reed. Later, when iNkosi checked on the lad through the same sky-opening, he found him wasting away from loneliness. Since iNkosi was himself the father of the boy, he decided to send the most beautiful young sky maiden to comfort him and be his wife. She too was lowered to earth by means of a cord and she found the youth by a banana plant. When the boy saw the girl, he realised from her great beauty that she had come from the lord-of-the-sky. He cut her cord as he had cut his own, whereupon iNkosi drew it back into heaven and closed the hole in the floor of the sky. Henceforth people could multiply on earth and were no longer lonely, seeking to return to heaven.

Berglund (1976:42) stresses that the creator god has sky connections, particularly with thunder and lightning. Further proof of these connections may be found in the ministry of people called 'heaven-herds' (*zinyanga zezulu/abeluzi bezulu*), who are believed to be responsible for diverting lightning and destructive weather. They are specially called to this task, not by the ancestral spirits, but in a direct encounter with the power of the sky, in which they narrowly escape death by lightning. Only males - who, irrespective of age, are known as 'boys' - are called to this profession. They undergo a prescribed initiation period before they begin the work to which they believe they were called.

Rainmakers, on the other hand, may be either male or female. It is understood, furthermore, that their gift for ending drought is received directly from the lord-of-the-sky. He alone is able to create rain. Although the ancestors may cause it to be withheld, they are powerless to make it fall.

In addition to the lord-of-the-sky - who is conceived of as male - a female element is represented by *Nomkubulwana*. Although she, the princess of heaven (*iNkosazana yeZulu*), is understood to be a maiden, she is nevertheless a type of earth mother in that she is associated with agriculture, spring rain and fertility. Beliefs concerning Nomkubulwana differ from one area to another, but she is understood variously to be the rainbow or a young girl (*intombi*). Her worship appears to be unrelated to ancestor veneration; young maidens celebrate the festival of *Nomdede* on a hillside in her honour. These ceremonies are held in springtime when mist commonly occurs on high places. During this time the girls make beer and temporarily take over the cattle-herding duties of the boys. Among some groups a special portion of the tribe's garden is reserved for Nomkubulwana. She may also be appealed to in times of drought or flood (Berglund 1976:64-68).

An actiological myth that is widely known among the Zulu attempts to explain the origins of death. In this myth uNkulunkulu is seen not only as existing in the beginning, but also as good. He desired that humans might live forever and sent the chameleon with a message granting them eternal life. Subsequently, however, it became necessary to send a message of mortality as well. This message he committed to the lizard. Unfortunately the chameleon, although he had a head start, dawdled along the way and the lizard arrived first to deliver his message which, by virtue of its priority, was effective and irrevocable. The analogy between this myth and the similar one among the San is readily apparent.

The exact nature of Zulu beliefs concerning the divine before the imposition of Christian beliefs is no longer clear. From even a cursory review of these myths, however, it seems reasonable to conclude that the people had conceptions of a transcendent creator who desired their happiness on earth. Closely related to beliefs concerning a Supreme Being are those concerning the continuing nature of the community in and through the ancestors (*amadlozi/amathongo*).

The extended community

Idlozi/Amadlozi

The Zulu belief in life after death is conceptualised in terms of certain notions concerning those who have recently died. The ancestors (*idlozi/amadlozi*), the shades (an anthropological term) or the living-dead (a term coined by John Mbiti), are remembered and continue to maintain a place in the family or tribal group for three or four generations in the case of commoners and somewhat longer in the case of royalty.

Just as life begins before the actual birth of an individual, so it fades gradually into obscurity. Older people in the kraal or village are already on their way to ancestorhood and are accorded due respect; they may be called amadlozi even before their death. Physical separation from the visible community is simply one more stage on the journey of life - a journey which starts with gradual admission to the community, leads through various stages of community participation, and ends with gradual departure to the spirit world.

Death in old age is considered natural. People are expected to live long enough to bear children and see their grandchildren. The death of such a person is referred to in words which imply continuing existence, albeit in an invisible form. Consequently an old person is not mourned excessively at death. The body is buried in the earth where the amadlozi are said to reside.

Throughout Africa the mere fact of death and burial does not enable a person to become an ancestor. Additional ritual actions must be performed. Among the Zulu, the *ukubuyisa idlozi* ceremony (bringing home of the spirit) is held by the deceased's descendants a year or two after his death. At this ritual, which is only performed for men who held positions of authority in the tribe, an ox is sacrificed and selected portions are given to the collective ancestors by placing them in the sacred area reserved for the amadlozi at the back of the hut. The recently deceased's name is included in the praise list of ancestors at this time and he is called upon to take his place among the protectors and defenders of his line. His eldest son, who presides over this ceremony, may drag a tree branch from the site of the grave to the entrance of the kraal, thus symbolically bringing the ancestor home (Hammond-Tooke 1974:328).

After this ceremony, the ancestral spirit can be expected to make himself known. He must be remembered from time to time as a member of the collective ancestral group. While all dead people go to the spirit world of shades, the ritual practices connected with the ukubuyisa idlozi of tribal authority figures seem to fulfil cultic requirements sufficiently to re-establish and maintain communication between the physical world and the spirit world where the ancestors reside.

If, however, a person dies prematurely - either without offspring or before reaching old age - witchcraft or sorcery is suspected. Such a death is described in terms indicative of a breaking off, and it is believed that the person could be enlisted as a spirit helper for evil purposes, rather than as an ancestor for purposes of protecting and benefiting the community.

The holistic world view which characterises Zulu thought is readily apparent in these ancestral beliefs. Well-being implies both unity and continuity. An individual exists to fulfil those obligations which support and maintain the group. The group takes precedence over the individual because the individual cannot exist apart from the group.

In Zulu thought, when someone is sick, it is the whole person - body and spirit - that is afflicted. No fundamental distinction is made between a person's visible, physical being and his or her invisible spirit being. The spirit which becomes the ancestor is viewed as the whole person and not merely as a part that has been separated from the body. Thus the term *idlozi*, as was indicated, may be applied both to very old people and to those who, having departed this visible realm, have returned as invisible beings.

In addition to idlozi or amadlozi, certain other names are used to refer to the spirits of dead people. When the ancestors appear in dreams, as they are fully expected to do, they may be referred to as *ithongo/amathongo*. The word *abaphansi* indicates those who dwell under the earth, a place where a shadowy existence is maintained, the reversal of physical life on earth. An ancestor who strikes a person in the shoulder (*uhlabo*) to cause him or her to become a diviner is called an *umhlabathi*. Ancestral shades may also be called *izithutha*, implying that they are unable to provide their own food and are thus dependent upon sacrificial meat (Berglund 1976:91).

There are numerous beliefs pertaining to the amadlozi, some localised and others which are more generally held. It is believed that they can declare their presence in the community by the appearance of certain snakes. These snakes do not die but merely shed their skins periodically, symbolising perpetual rebirth. Such snakes are also regarded as portents that assure female fertility and help women in childbirth. If snakes are seen near a fresh burial site, it is immediately understood that the person's idlozi has returned. A lizard may also indicate the presence of an idlozi.

Ancestral shades or spirits can make themselves known by other unusual signs, such as abnormal behaviour in an antelope or unusual events during the birth of a child. They may make their disapproval felt by inflicting sickness on individuals, barrenness on women, or misfortunes such as the loss of a job or a poor harvest. They may communicate their approval by sending prosperity and fertility to both fields and people.

When adverse events or signs occur, it is necessary to consult a diviner to ascertain which ancestral shade is responsible so as to determine what sacrifice is expected. One could also offer a sacrifice directly to the ancestor assumed to be responsible, without consulting a diviner.

Most commonly, ancestors reveal themselves through dreams. It is expected that people will dream - in fact, it is cause for great concern if they do not. Although dreams can be caused by witchcraft or sorcery, they are normally considered to be a channel of communication between the departed and those still living in the visible community.

Three places in the hut have ancestral associations. These are the *umsamo* right at the back of the hut, the hearth and the doorway. The umsamo is a cool dark spot where snakes (ancestors) frequently go and where special pieces of sacrifical meat are placed for them. In addition cooking pots are left unscraped on the hearth for the amadlozi to eat clean. A special piece of thatch may be placed at the crown of the arched doorway, between the doorposts, in recognition of the ancestors. Both the hearth and the doorway have sexual associations, and ancestors are believed to be involved in reproduction and childbirth.

As mentioned previously, a close relationship exists between people and their cattle. This affiliation is extended to include the ancestors. As with the hut, there are three places in the cattle enclosure which are sacred to the amadlozi: the gateway, a pit in the centre of the enclosure where grain is stored, and the far interior.

However, as spirit beings the ancestors are not restricted to certain places. It is understood that they continue to exist under the earth; but they are also invisibly present in the homestead and the cattle enclosure, and even return in the visible guise of their progeny. Their presence may also be assumed in a person's head, back, sexual organs and especially in the shoulder blades.

Sacrifices are offered in honour of the spirits of the dead to avert disaster (for example during childbirth), to secure a blessing (as at the building of a new kraal or when going off to battle), or as an act of thanksgiving (for health, ripe old age or military victory). The ancestors are included in all actions where the well-being of the community is at issue.

Beliefs concerning the ancestral shades are closely interwoven with those concerning the diviners, known as *izangoma*.

Izinyanga and izangoma

People usually maintain a respectful distance from the ancestors, except in certain circumstances when their very close presence is required. Then a person may enter into a state called 'brooding' (*ukufukamela* - the word used to refer to a broody hen). Brooding changes the person into a different individual. A widow, for example, can become mentally deranged through excessive brooding, or a person may become a diviner. White clay smeared on a person's face is an indication of the brooding of the spirits. Four distinct, definable rites relate to this condition: abstention from washing in water; a gall-bladder fixed onto the person's head; abstention from cutting the hair and from the paring of one or more nails; and the putting aside of all finery or cosmetics. Brooding must be controlled lest it cause madness (Berglund 1976:127-134).

As indicated, there are strong mythological links between the ancestral and diviner belief systems. It is believed that the izinyanga first taught humankind about the existence and proper care of the amadlozi. At the same time izinyanga are believed to have received their call or designation to the profession from the ancestral spirits.

This call comes in the form of an illness characterised by body pains, uncontrollable nervous twitchings and periods of dissociation or trance. The 'called' person is much given to strange, obscure and frightening dreams and is described as having a 'soft head'. During this initial illness, the individual thus singled out from the ordinary community begins to waste away and has little appetite for food. His or her body is said to become *dungekile* from excessive dreaming, as water becomes muddy when a puddle is stirred up. The person is awakened at night by ancestral shades, since they communicate best immediately after the family has gone to sleep at night or early in the morning before they awake. If the person does not agree to become a diviner and attempts to debar the spirits, it is likely that he or she will never become well again. Other symptoms of this initial period include loss of hair, excessive yawning and sneezing, weeping and/or singing songs during the night - which, of course, is disruptive to the entire community and makes everyone aware of the troubling presence of the ancestral spirits (Callaway 1970:260-263).

Both men and women may be called to be diviners, but among the Zulu the majority are women. Men who become diviners dress like women especially during the initiation period. The first step is to take the sufferer to a practising isangoma to determine which ancestral spirits are responsible for the call. If the sickness is diagnosed as *ukuthwasa*, it must then be decided whether to attempt to debar the spirit or to accept it (*ukuvuma idlozi*). The latter course of action is the surest way to restore health. The person then proceeds to become apprenticed to a senior practising diviner and undergoes lengthy training. This includes learning the uses and manner of securing medicines, as well as methods of inducing trance, especially by means of dancing. The training has two main purposes. The first is the restoration of the novice's health; the second is adaptation to the life of a diviner. The novice must learn to adjust to the condition known as brooding without becoming mentally disordered and she must acquire the knowledge required for her work of divination.

Various taboos, particularly regarding certain foods, obtain during the apprenticeship and the novice is to some extent excluded from the normal life of the community. The period of training may last from one to two years. At the end of it the isangoma's embarkation on her new life is marked by an initiation ceremony. The association with the ancestors is especially emphasised, for instance by the ritual slaughter and sacrifice of goats to the amadlozi. The isangoma subsequently wears the gall bladders of the sacrificial goats in her hair, perhaps as a sort of professional 'diploma' but also as a symbol of her association with the ancestors. The skin of the goat is cut into strips which are worn across the shoulders and fastened at the back and the front as a part of the new isangoma's costume. Also at the initiation ceremony, songs of the profession are sung and feats of skill performed, for instance finding things that people have hidden. The new isangoma has to catch a wild animal whose vertebrae will later be made into a necklace, forming another part of her costume. Gifts are presented to her. This ritual marks the end of the *ukuthwasa* or coming-out period.

Since the ancestors selected this person for her mediatory work by 'stabbing' her in her shoulders, this part of the isangoma's body remains forever sensitive. It is where the ancestors dwell.

Various attempts have been made to categorise those people who specialise in the healing of both individuals and the community by restoring wholeness. A primary distinction is that between ancestrally designated diviners or mediators and those whose work consists in supplying herbal and other medicines. The latter have not necessarily been directly called to the profession by the ancestral shades.

Bryant's (1966:13) relatively early classification suggested that a distinction be made between the *inyanga yokwelapha*, who is primarily concerned with healing by means of herbs and medicines, and the *inyanga yokubhula* who is primarily concerned with divination. Among the latter are found the isangoma and the *isanusi* (who 'smell out' people guilty of witchcraft). Nowadays these categorical divisions are often blurred and many izinyanga (doctors) are izangoma (diviners) as well. It is, however, primarily the isangoma who, as a diviner/mediator, plays a religious role because of her calling and continued relationship with the ancestors.

Throughout the isangoma's life and practice she is believed to be in direct communication with the ancestors, and hence with the entire spirit realm as conceived by the Zulu. Whenever illness or impending disaster troubles the village, people go to consult an isangoma. If they are not satisfied with the diagnosis of the first one consulted, they may seek a second opinion, sometimes travelling considerable distances to do so. People who come for consultation wait for the diviner to tell them why they have come. They indicate the accuracy of the isangoma's explanation by striking the ground with branches, softly or not at all if it is incorrect, and loudly if the reason given is valid.

The doctor then proceeds to name the illness and to prescribe certain measures. These may include the slaughter of an animal to appease the ancestors or a visit to a herbalist. Today most diviners are herbalists as well and the required medicines may be obtained directly from them. It is customary for a doctor to acknowledge the help of the ancestors at the place where he digs for his herbal medicines (Callaway 1970:219).

Diviners may specialise in various functions. The *izanusi* are specialists in finding lost property; other specialists are characterised as stick diviners, bone diviners and ventriloquists (*abalozi*).

Remember, however, that all are persons who serve the community by virtue of their special relationship with the ancestral shades and thus with the entire spirit realm. It is not unreasonable to view the amadlozi/izangoma complex as representing the core of Zulu religious beliefs. The importance of the ancestors as mediators needs to be emphasised. They are both accessible and in touch with Zulu affairs, whereas the Supreme Being is difficult to conceptualise and thus remains vague. The izangoma then provide a direct line of communication to the ancestors who are the official protectors of the community.

Likewise izangoma are generally caring individuals who are keenly aware of the need for a holistic approach to illnesses. They are specialists in diagnosing and prescribing cures for 'cultural illnesses'. Their importance to the Zulu people is witnessed not only by the fact that their services are sought even by those who have, in many respects, moved into the mainstream of modern, westernised societies, but also by the office of the prophet/healer in the numerous indigenous churches of South Africa. This office is a reflection of the need which the Zulu people recognise for a person who can stand as the mystical or religious connective between the physical and the spiritual realms, uniting them into one complete whole. The izangoma assure essential vitality and continuation of health for individuals, and by extension for a group.

Good health consists not only of a healthy body, but a healthy situation of everything that concerns a person. Good health means the harmonious working and coordination of a person's universe (Ngubane 1977:28).

The izangoma diagnose and prescribe, in consultation with the ancestors, so that health may be maintained or restored. The office of the isangoma presents a model which provides a focal point for the positive health and unifying orientation of the community in both a societal and a spiritual sphere.

Lineage leaders

The isangoma is not the only person qualified and responsible to maintain communication with the ancestors. The leader of the visible community, the senior kinsman or lineage head, also performs this role. He could be viewed as a priest or cultic and ritual leader. He is responsible not only for assuring the maintenance of good relationships with the ancestors (e g by making appropriate sacrifices), but also for all cultic arrangements. Dates of ritual killings must be arranged with him and he has to see that all parties involved are notified so that they can, if at all possible, be present.

In a manner of speaking the chief, who is primarily the political head of a number of family groups or lineages, stands at the apex of the religious system - thus in a sense the tribal high priest. His relationship to the spirit community is vouchsafed by his position as head of the ruling family as well as by the mystical aura attached to his high political office. Only the chief can perform propitiatory sacrifices to the ancestors of dead chiefs in times of tribal emergency, so that he forms a special link with the spirit realm.

By extension, the king possesses even greater religious potency by virtue of his position as head of the entire nation, with all the mystical power emanating from this exalted office. A Zulu king thus fulfils an especially powerful national function which is more than merely political (Hammond-Tooke 1974:350).

Ubuthakathi

For the Zulu the ideal life is achieved when harmony and health prevail throughout the community. This state is realised when fields, animals and humans are fertile and when people's lives are marked by respectful care for one another, good neighbourliness, generosity and sexual morality. Whenever the balance of life is disrupted through ill health, infertility or other misfortunes, a cause is sought. While ordinary illnesses and old age are accepted, other disruptive forces are viewed as evil and have to be explained before a remedy can be sought. Generally there are two major sources of abnormal illnesses. The first is the ancestors, in which case the disruptions are regarded as punishment for some breach of duty and are usually not fatal. The situation may be remedied by performing the neglected duty. This often entails preparing a sacrificial meal in honour of the offended ancestor.

The second source is more greatly feared and not so readily disposed of. This agent of disruption is wholly malevolent and is conceptualised in terms of witchcraft and sorcery, either of which may be described by the term *ubuthakathi*.

Anger, which inevitably occurs in human situations, is greatly feared. It must be controlled, for if it is not, it will express itself in evil actions. This is the essence of ubuthakathi. Measures are therefore taken to bring anger to the surface. People are encouraged to confess their ill-feelings at community gatherings. Diviners are quick to pinpoint the seeds of malicious anger in individuals; they also identify more advanced stages which have already become manifest in witchcraft or sorcery. Witchcraft thus represents the dark, malevolent feelings that lie in human hearts - hatred, envy, vengefulness and malice.

Whereas men may be accused of sorcery for using medicines for wicked (selfish, antisocial) purposes, those accused of witchcraft are usually women (*abathakathi*). It is believed that they do their evil work at night. They may or may not be aware of their own nocturnal activities. It is understood that they habitually do evil deeds, directed not so much against the community at large as against particular individuals who, for whatever reason, have become the targets of their anger. As might be expected, accusations of witchcraft often arise amongst in-laws in family situations, especially when living conditions are crowded or unsatisfactory, thus breeding irritation and misunderstanding.

The modus operandi of the witch is that her evil spirit leaves her earthly body and congregates after dark with other evil spirits. Nakedness, cannibalism and invisibility are associated with witchcraft. Animals, especially the baboon and the wild cat, may be employed to carry out evil deeds and an association is maintained with such mythical evil creatures as the *utikoloshe* (which has sexual connotations), the *impundulu* or lightning bird and zombis (*imikhovu*), that witches are believed to raise up from dead bodies to do their wicked bidding.

When witches are discovered and declared, they must be destroyed in order that the community may be healed. Although punishment by death is no longer prevalent among the Zulu, as it was in former times, the belief in witchcraft persists. Traditionally punishment by death was considered the only way to deal with sin which arises from hidden anger. The sentence could be impalement on a stake, being tied up in a skin and thrown to the crocodiles, being clubbed to death or being thrown over a cliff. The witch's home was then razed to the ground and destroyed by burning. Thus negative elements which destroy social balance and harmony have to be sought out and eliminated. Only the isangoma is in a position to guide the community in determining the necessary restorative measures.

Ritual action

Social congruence and well-being are also maintained by means of ritual action. Hammond-Tooke (1974:351-356) categorises ritual action as either kinship or community rites. Because kinship rituals relate to family matters, they have strong connections with ancestral spirits. Ritual actions may be performed at each transitional stage in the cycle of life - birth, puberty, marriage and death. An example is the ukubuyisa, when a deceased family member returns as a spirit.

We have mentioned that, in order to avert evil or to appease the ancestors in cases of misfortune, it is necessary periodically to slaughter an animal for a ritual meal in honour of the ancestors. These may be considered piacular sacrifices or rituals and, in all cases, the accent is on unity and accord within the family group. In such a ritual sacrifice, the officiant praises the ancestors loudly at the cattle kraal before telling them which beast he is about to present to them. After this the animal is thrown to the ground and stabbed with a sacrificial spear. The animal is expected to bellow loudly, whereupon the officiant proclaims, 'Cry, ox of the amadlozi!' and again identifies the ancestors by name. The dead animal is then skinned and the first portions, including the fourth stomach (which has to be burnt) and other selected pieces, are placed in the umsamo at the back of the great hut for the ancestors to lick. The remainder of the animal is ritually distributed among those present and eaten that same day. The remains (skin and bones) are burned. When the ritual is performed on behalf of someone who is ill, the patient is smeared with the gall of the animal, so that the ancestral spirits will 'lick' and thereby cure the person. The sacrifice, in the form of a communal meal, thus unites the living with the dead.

Loyalty and unity are essential not only for the kinship group, but also for the tribe as a whole, which in essence has an existence of its own. Community rituals extend beyond the confines of the family and require participation and attendance by the entire tribe. They include such ceremonies as rain rituals, rituals to protect the ripening crops and the festival of first fruits.

Among the Zulu, rain rituals are often presided over by the tribal chief rather than by a diviner. A dark skinned animal is slaughtered, perhaps by analogy with the desired black rain clouds. Crops of maize may be protected from blight or hail by rituals in which young girls, clad only in their beaded aprons, run through the fields. A cardinal communal ritual is the annual first-fruits or harvest festival, which is also considered to be a means of strengthening the chief and his army. The chief or king is expected to take the first mouthful of the newly harvested crops and, in a ritual act of thanksgiving, spit it upon the ground. This ceremony formerly included the doctoring of the army with strong medicines in a series of ritual actions, such as the killing of a bull by unarmed warriors and sanctioned criticism of the chief or king.

The religious orientation of the Zulu people may be said to comprise two major divisions. There is a prevailing conception of the divine manifested in belief in a supreme creator sky-god and, possibly, other lesser deities (e.g. Nombukhulwana). There is an equally strong belief in the living community, both the visible and the invisible (as represented by the ancestors). Unity and wholeness must be maintained within the community so that life may be sustained. Proper recognition is therefore accorded to senior dignitaries, both living and dead. Anger is a disruptive force and must be dealt with. The mechanisms instituted for the maintenance of wholeness are the diviner-mediators and ritualised actions.

This chapter merely scratches the surface of the Zulu's religious orientation to life. It is sincerely hoped, however, that it will stimulate further independent study.

SUGGESTED READING

Berglund, A-I 1976. *Zulu thought-patterns and symbolism*. Claremont: Philip.

Hammond-Tooke, W D 1989. *Rituals and medicines: indigenous healing in South Africa*. Johannesburg: Donker.

Ngubane, H 1977. *Body and mind in Zulu medicine: an ethnography of health and disease in Nyuswa-Zulu thought and practice*. London: Academic Press.

CHAPTER 4

The Shona-speaking people of Zimbabwe

In this chapter the heterogeneity of Shona religion is considered by way of a review of beliefs concerning the high-god, Mwari; spirit possession by *midzimu, mashavi* and *ngozi* spirits; the role of the *nganga* and the *muroyi*; and the importance of the individual's status in his or her community.

HISTORICAL REVIEW

Archaeological evidence seems to suggest that as long as 8 000 years ago a Bushman culture predominated in the area that forms the focus of this chapter. Although historians are unable to tell us exactly what occurred in those early times, it is possible to piece together an approximate picture by combining artifacts from archaeological discoveries with oral traditions and written European accounts of more recent events. The most outstanding feature to emerge from such a reconstruction is the extremely long and varied history of this area.

The first people to inhabit the land known today as Zimbabwe were the Khoisan hunters who led a semi-nomadic life. Prior to the nineteenth century there were large-scale migrations of Africans moving southward over the continent. The first of these probably reached Zimbabwe in about the second century (100 CE). The invaders were Bantu-speaking people (early iron age) who settled on the high fertile plateau between the Limpopo and the Zambesi

Rivers. Thus the natural drop of the land towards the ocean on the east and the Kalahari desert on the west marked the borders of their territory. The area was rich in minerals such as iron, gold and copper, to which these resourceful people gained access by means of surface mining.

About the same time that these early Bantu people, who were agriculturalists and cattle owners, began to settle in the area, the Khoisan gradually drifted out of it. There is no evidence to suggest that they were forcibly driven from the area and it is reasonable to assume that they simply departed so as to pursue their chosen way of life in peace.

Only some of the Bantu-speaking people who entered the Zimbabwe area remained there. It has been suggested that others may have continued southward to form the Nguni, Sotho, Tsonga, Venda and Chopi peoples inhabiting other areas of southern Africa. Those who remained were familiar with iron-smelting and able to make such iron tools as hoes and axes. At an early date they may have engaged in gold and ivory trade with Muslim merchants from the east coast (Bourdillon 1976:20).

About the year 1000 (c 900 on the plateau and c 1100 in the north), another group of immigrants replaced the first Bantu or early iron age people. These spoke Shona and seem to have been closely related to the present-day Karanga group of Shona speakers.

According to Beach (1980:36) Shona history in the period which followed may be analysed in terms of four major political units. These are: (a) the loosely knit states around Great Zimbabwe prior to the sixteenth century; (b) the Torwa state that dominated the southwestern area from the late fifteenth to the late seventeenth century, when it was superseded by (c) the Changamire-Rozvi state which lasted until the 1840s; and (d) in the north the Mutapa state which existed concurrently with the Zimbabwean culture from at least the fifteenth to the nineteenth century.

Undoubtedly the most commonly recognised culture today is that of early Zimbabwe, renowned for its technique of building stone walls from layers of (exfoliated) granite. The magnificent ruins of Great Zimbabwe remain to this day as a testimonial to the skill of these remarkable people.

But by the mid-fifteenth century, when the Portuguese arrived on the scene, Great Zimbabwe had ceased to be a major trading centre of the Karanga. Intermarriage had probably occurred between some of the earlier iron age Bantu people and the later Shona-speaking Bantu, and these people's descendants gradually moved further away from their original settlements. According to Bourdillon (1976:24,25) the Portuguese, upon their arrival, found only dwindling remains of what had once been a powerful dynasty controlled by the great Mutapa. The Portuguese nonetheless continued to support successive rulers of this dynasty until the defeat of the last of the Mutapas at their hands in 1917.

Beach (1980:80), on the other hand, concludes that the legend of a great Mutapa who dwelt at Zimbabwe is a fabrication. He indicates that the entire area known as the Mutapa state was a loose conglomerate of villages and chiefdoms which continued to exist after the decline of Great Zimbabwe. Very likely an abundance of cattle contributed to the abandonment of Great Zimbabwe as people moved with their herds in search of better grazing.

During this entire period there was a flourishing trade with people from the coastal areas of Mozambique. The Shona exchanged their gold, obtained from surface mining, for highly prized cloth and beads from India.

The history of the southern Shona territory is difficult to trace with any degree of accuracy. It is known, however, that at the southwestern end of the plateau there were five successive political systems. Zimbabwean culture was succeeded by the Torwa state, based on the Khami culture. In the late seventeenth century this, in turn, was replaced by the Changamire-Rozvi state which survived until the mid-nineteenth century, when the Ndebele imposed their language and culture upon the people. Between 1650 and 1850 there was a considerable amount of settling and resettling of the area in question, so that Tsonga, Venda, Sotho and Nguni peoples have all left their mark upon the southern Shona language and culture (Beach 1980:189, 190).

The Changamire-Rozvi people (1600s to 1800s) controlled the trade with the Portuguese for a long time and probably established the previously existing cult of the high-god Mwari in the Matopo Hills (Daneel 1971:81). Although the Changamire-Rozvi state was eventually overcome by the invading (Zulu-speaking) Ndebele from the south under Mzilikazi, the Mwari high-god cult not only survived but became a central feature of the religion of the new invaders. It also exerted an influence on other people who settled in nearby areas.

At about this time the British entered the scene and mistakenly judged the Shona to be no more than a bunch of squabbling petty chieftaincies living in subjection to the Ndebele. As the truth of Shona history emerged by degrees, this verdict has consistently been refuted. A further injustice was done to these aristocratic people when the British and the Portuguese agreed among themselves on the boundaries of Rhodesia and Portuguese East Africa. These boundaries of European contrivance often cut right through existing Shona chiefdoms. Many Shona were removed from their land to make way for white farmers. Some chiefdoms were completely broken up and their inhabitants resettled on less suitable land (Bourdillon 1976:31). Nevertheless it must be conceded that this period of the colonial settlement of Rhodesia gave a general boost to Shona cultural development, launching them into an era of material progress and change that culminated in the progressive modern nation of present-day Zimbabwe.

Probably the name 'Shona' was originally a derogatory title given by the Ndebele to the people we are about to review. The Shona people use it only as a means of distinguishing themselves from other language groups. While primarily a linguistic classification, it is also a convenient term to designate a people who not only share a language, but also have certain cultural and, to some extent, historical links.

The chiefdoms or dialect groups referred to in this chapter are the Karanga, the Zezuru of central Shona country and the Korekore peoples to the north. Although the Ndau and the Manyika peoples' boundaries extend into Mozambique, those residing in present-day Zimbabwe are not excluded. The Kalanga group which has largely been absorbed by the Ndebele culture is not taken into consideration.

CULTURAL REVIEW

Many Shona people today live in the large metropolitan areas of Zimbabwe. Others still dwell in rural or semirural areas where they maintain the traditional Shona life-style which is the focus of this chapter.

The boundaries between religion and culture are not always clearly discernible in African traditional communities. One reason for this is the close family bond characterised by the phrase *mwana wamai* (mother's child). This bond extends beyond the confines of the visible family to embrace those still to be born and, even more significantly, those who have passed from the physical to the spirit realm, thereby becoming ancestors. The closeness and the concomitant binding obligations of Shona family life extend to village and ward divisions as well.

Traditionally Mashonaland was composed of a patchwork of chieftaincies or clan divisions called *nyika* (land/chiefdom). In each nyika the dominant clan forms the nucleus of the ruling class. It can, however, include numerous variations of other, unrelated clan groups. Members of the same clan have the same totem and ceremonial greetings and are permitted to marry only within the subclan grouping. Each nyika consists of districts or wards (*dunhu*) which, in turn, comprise villages (*musha*) consisting of several homesteads. Every person has ceremonial obligations which pertain both to their nuclear family and to these extended kinship networks.

The village or musha is the immediate unit around which daily life revolves. It is composed of a nuclear family consisting of a man, his wife or wives, their children, his parents, his brothers, their wives and children, and his unmarried sisters. The immediate ancestors (*midzimu*) protect and guide the members of the village. In turn, proper respect must be shown both to the ancestors and to fellow villagers. This takes the form of actions that have both ritual and practical significance, such as providing bridewealth for marriageable women and seeing that totem marriage regulations are observed.

The ideal Shona (*munhu chaiye*, 'real person') is humble, kind, ready to share with others and never greedy for more than is his or her due in life. He or she adheres to those time-honoured ritual observances which bind together all members of the group, both living and dead (Gelfand 1981:7).

An ancestrally sanctioned day of rest (*chisi*) is observed when no one is permitted to work in the fields. The chief is understood to be the father of the nyika. From time to time he holds court (*dare*) to settle disputes which may have arisen. He also supervises four annual rituals: petitions for rain, planting of seeds, thanksgiving for the appearance of green crops and thanksgiving for the harvest.

In view of the considerable correspondence between Shona culture and religion, it is appropriate to pay due attention to the latter. Shona religion will be analysed in terms of four interrelated categories: belief in Mwari; belief in a spirit realm; belief in good and bad medicine; and belief in the continuing community.

THE RELIGIOUS ORIENTATION OF THE SHONA PEOPLE

Belief in Mwari

Like the majority of African people, the Shona believe in a supreme creator. It is not possible to ascertain how clear a concept of the high-god existed before the arrival of Christian missionaries and there are plenty of arguments on both sides. Certainly if the Mwari cult, which is firmly entrenched in the southern part of Mashonaland, is accepted as representative of beliefs in the deity throughout the territory, the concept of a remote god (*deus otiosus* or *deus remotus*) must be viewed with some reservation. In spite of the fact that he is approached indirectly by individuals through designated spirit mediums and that few rituals are actually directed to him, he can nevertheless be viewed as an active god, present not only in the mythical past of creation, but also among his people today.

Of course, the possibility exists that the Mwari cult has taken on an importance and structure which it would not have assumed but for outside (European and Ndebele) pressures. However, most of the following statements concerning beliefs about god among the Shona are based on what we know about the god of the Matopo Hills (Mwari). Our source for most of this information is the work of M L Daneel, who not only researched the Mwari cult extensively but was probably the first non-Shona to be granted permission to attend an oracular session in the Matopos. His findings and conclusions regarding the organisation of the cult have been published in a book, *The god of the Matopo Hills: an essay on the Mwari cult in Rhodesia* (1970).

Mwari is the final authority above and beyond the ancestors, and as such he must be approached indirectly through mediums representing ancestral spirits. He controls fertility - both human and agricultural - throughout Shona country. He is regarded as the ultimate source of rain and his help is requested in times of drought or when some other form of national crisis threatens. He is expected to advise on the course of action to be followed in such times of crisis.

Myths or legends about Mwari are rare and, apart from ceremonies at his shrine in the Matopo Hills, few rituals are performed to appease or placate him. Nevertheless, according to Bourdillon (1976:321), he is understood to be ultimately responsible for everything, including the weather, forests and fields; even individual personality traits are attributed to him. He is not viewed as a god exclusively for the Shona, but as the god of all humankind, both white and black. This follows because not only does rain fall on all people alike, but it is known that the things regarded as his particular property (e g wild fruit, honey, game) should not be withheld from outsiders.

It would be presumptuous for individuals to trouble Mwari with their personal problems which are the responsibility of family or village ancestors, but all events with far-reaching effects fall under his jurisdiction. Even events that occur in the natural order of things - such as thunder and lightning, the death of old people and certain 'natural' illnesses where witchcraft is not suspected - are attributed to Mwari.

Numerous praise names are given to Mwari. The most popular is *Dzivaguru* (the Great Pool), which refers to his ability to send rain. He is also known as *Chidziva ahopo* (the little pool that is always there). As *Nyadenga* or *Dedza* he is lord of the sky; as *Musikavanhu*, creator of the people; as *Chikara*, the one who inspires awe; and as *Mutangakugara*, the one who existed at the beginning (Daneel 1971:81; Bourdillon 1976:321).

The names given to Mwari indicate certain attitudes or beliefs concerning him. Some of these are self-evident, such as his connection with the sky and his role in creation. Others may be less obvious to outsiders but are nevertheless readily apparent to the Shona themselves. The names *Dziva, Mbuya* (grandmother) and *Zendere*, for example, represent the female aspect of Mwari, while such names as *Sororezhou* (elephant head or father) and *Wokumusoro* point to his male aspect. He is, therefore, both male and female. The title *Nyadenga* refers to his sky connections, while *Dzivanguru* indicates his association with the earth or the depths. As the author of creation Mwari is therefore both a male god of light and a female goddess of fertility (Daneel 1971:82).

While the ordinary ethics of justice and right living are upheld by the ancestors, it is believed that Mwari personally punishes those who do not observe chisi, the ancestral day of rest which, therefore, belongs to him.

As was previously stated, Mwari can only be approached indirectly through senior lineage ancestors (*mhondoro*, which name means 'ancestral lion spirit' and is likewise applied to the human mediator, or *varudzi*) or by special messengers sent to his shrine to receive directions for the community through the oracular Voice of Mwari which speaks from a cave. This means that, for the individual Shona, Mwari is somewhat remote. His principal shrine is at Matonjeni in the Matopo Hills, at present in Ndebele territory. There a number of hereditary cultic officials conduct regular annual ceremonies, such as the petition for rain and thanksgiving for the harvest. The chief officials are a high priest and a high priestess (his sister) who communicate directly with the oracle; an elderly woman who is married into the high-priestly family and who provides the audible voice of the oracle; and an elderly man, related by lineage to the high priest, who serves as keeper of the shrine. In addition there are lesser officials who reside at the shrine either permanently or for extended periods (Daneel 1971:86).

In community crises (drought, appointment of a new chief, acceptance of a mhondoro, etc) an official delegation can be sent from a village or ward to ask guidance from the 'Voice'. The directions given usually corroborate the traditional teachings and established practices of the group in question. Contributions to support the shrine, its officials and the ritual ceremonies which are held there are collected from the various villages and wards by the senior tribal official or by the cultic messenger of the group.

It stands to reason that the high-god cult is strongest in the southern part of Mashonaland. Farther north the mhondoro cults take on some of the characteristics of the high-god cult of the Matopo Hills. The high-god cult should not be viewed in isolation from the warp and weft of Shona religion generally. Significant in this regard is the point made by Daneel (1970:55) that the entire Matonjeni community is organised as a physical replica concretely symbolising the Shona view of the entire spirit world.

The logical next step is to review Shona beliefs concerning a general world of spirits, since Shona religion - like all African religion - cannot be fully described purely with reference to belief in a supreme being.

Belief in a spirit realm

An outstanding characteristic of Shona religion is its openness to communication with an invisible realm of spirits. There are certain differences of emphasis among the various clan groupings throughout Mashonaland. This is to be expected in view of normal variations attributable to geographical and historical factors, which account for the relatively high degree of heterogeneity observable in Shona culture. The comments which follow are therefore only a general summary of Shona beliefs in this regard.

Spirit possession is generally viewed positively in Shona culture. It is a frequent occurrence and is understood as a means of maintaining intercourse with an invisible spirit realm. Thus the spirit mediums pertaining to the Mwari cult are recognised, among other things, by their ability to enter into states of trance (or possession).

There are three major types of spirits which have intercourse with human beings. These are the *midzimu* or ancestral spirits, the *mashavi* or alien spirits and the *ngozi* or angry spirits of vengeance.

Generally the midzimu are understood to be protective spirits responsible for the welfare of the family (*midzimu yapamusha*) or of the tribe (mhondoro spirits). They are mediators who speak to the people on behalf of the spirit world through dreams, illness or misfortune, or through individuals specially called to be their mediating human counterparts (*svikiro* or spirit mediums). They can become troublesome or angry, even hurting or afflicting their living relatives if they are disregarded, but their primary function is one of guardianship.

Mashavi are foreign spirits of people who have died in Shona territory without proper burial in their own land; but they may include spirits of animals such as the baboon, or nature spirits such as water spirits. More commonly, however, they are the spirits of neighbouring tribesmen or of whites. Their presence is made known when they attempt to possess or inhabit the living. Usually it is understood that the shavi comes to bestow some particular skill on his host, although many mashavi seemingly desire primarily to dance. People possessed by mashavi spirits often unite to form cults according to the skills with which they are endowed. Dancing and entertainment are common features of the gatherings of these possession cults.

In addition to these primarily benevolent, albeit demanding, spirits, there are spirits of vengeance, the ngozi, who represent evil and ill-will not dealt with in this life. They are harmful spirits, usually of people who were murdered or children killed by witchcraft or people who received no proper burial, and so on. It would seem that the Shona subscribe to the idea that the evils which people do live after them and return as ngozi to harm and claim vengeance. Only the nganga can deal with ngozi spirits, and then only on the understanding that it entails possible danger.

Ngozi spirits seek to afflict or do harm, even to the point of death, to individuals, families or entire villages. Midzimu and mashavi spirits, on the other hand, merely seek a living host whom they can inhabit or possess, subsequently making their presence felt whenever they so desire. Very often midzimu spirits wish to communicate directly with their offspring, to which end they select a member of the family as their mouthpiece. A person thus chosen is called a *svikiro*.

The initial sign that a spirit desires to enter a person is a persistent illness which does not respond to ordinary treatment. The person so afflicted may exhibit strange behaviour and will certainly go into periods of trance when he or she seems to speak with another's voice. If the family suspects that a spirit is attempting to gain entrance to the sick person's body, they consult a nganga, who is expected to give positive identification. If the family has no ancestral medium, and especially if the family is facing some kind of crisis, the diagnosis is generally that the person has been chosen as a svikiro by a mudzimu. Otherwise the spirit seeking a host may be diagnosed as a shavi spirit whose identity is made known by certain compulsive behavioural characteristics.

Once the spirit has been identified, the immediate family of the afflicted person holds a feast during which the chosen person recognises and accepts the invading spirit. Since it is believed that the spirit may leave and seek a new host if this recognition is not perpetuated, an annual feast is held in its honour.

When a spirit medium is chosen by a mhondoro tribal ancestral spirit, the person thus chosen is treated as the mhondoro himself and addressed accordingly. It is understandable that he thereby gains considerable status in society and is called upon to give guidance in the selection of a new chief when necessary. He also figures prominently in rain ceremonies, since the mhondoro as the ultimate owner of the nyika can give or withhold rain. Requests to the mhondoro ancestral founder are not made by the mhondoro host, however, but by the head of the clan.

Apart from becoming a svikiro or simply the host of a shavi spirit, a possessed person afflicted by a strange illness may be diagnosed by the nganga as having been chosen by either a midzimu or a shavi spirit which is seeking to continue its service to the community by granting the gift of healing. In this case the person so chosen becomes a nganga who practises 'good' medicine and is of positive value to society.

Belief in good and bad medicine

The Shona believe that there are both good and evil spirits which have supernatural power to benefit or to destroy life. The nganga has an abundance of power which should be directed towards the good of the community, while the muroyi usurps power for destructive purposes. The muroyi is the antisocial individual who causes division within society. The purpose of the nganga, on the other hand, is to unite and maintain solidarity in the community. Nevertheless, since the power at issue is supernatural, both the nganga and the muroyi are feared. Besides, not all nganga achieve the goal of spreading well-being. A nganga, in one way or another, may be diverted to pursue selfish ends and thus be suspected of witchcraft. Despite this the paradigm which defines the role for a nganga implies positive value, while that of a witch implies negative value for both individuals and the community as a whole.

The first signs of a 'calling' to practise as a nganga are similar to those of spirit possession generally, although the person concerned often has healing dreams in which he or she (a nganga may be either male or female) is instructed, for example, on where to dig for particular herbal remedies. Often this calling runs in families, since it is usually the ancestral spirit of a former healer who seeks a host so as to continue its activities. It may, however, also happen to someone who does not have a nganga ancestor, especially if it is a shavi healing spirit seeking a living host.

Once the illness has been diagnosed by a practising nganga as having been caused by a healing spirit, and the spirit has been accepted by the person and the family, the individual undergoes training with a practising nganga. Occasionally a person does not have the normal illness and dreams which precede a call to become a healer, but simply undergoes training. These instances are not common, however, as the gift of healing is understood to be a spiritual one which must be passed on to living hosts. Upon completion of the training period, a feast is held by the family of the novice nganga and the healer then sets up practice.

The Shona recognise that many illnesses have ordinary causes and these are treated by home remedies or, nowadays, taken to Western doctors. Only prolonged illnesses which do not respond to ordinary measures are taken to a nganga for treatment. Apart from physical complaints, misfortune or bad luck is viewed as an illness to be treated. People may also seek protection for a long journey which they are about to take, or for success in their work, marriage, etc. Those things which seem to have no human explanation are understood as having an invisible cause. Since the main function of ngangas is to communicate with the spirit world, they are best suited to deal with these matters. The first step in healing is to ascertain the cause, whereafter appropriate measures must be taken and proper remedies administered.

The nganga sets about discovering the cause of the problem by divination. In general divination is concerned with past behaviour rather than predicting the future. Although ngangas use various methods, the most common are throwing the divining dice and spirit possession, or a combination of the two.

Divining dice (*hakata*) are usually rectangular pieces of wood or bone, although shells are used in the northern part of Mashonaland. A set of hakata consists of six pieces, and a diviner usually owns at least three sets which, when thrown, must agree before a final diagnosis can be made. Dice made from wood are about ten by two to three centimetres with a pattern carved on one side. When the patterned side faces upward it gives a positive identification to the problem. Each of the possible seven combinations of the dice has a name and a rather vague range of meanings, depending on the background to the question. These meanings are sufficiently well-known to the doctor, and often also to the patient, who may be asked to perform the first throw of the dice. The patient is thus involved in the cause-finding process. The dice have to be treated with medicine from time to time so that they will be able to 'see' properly and give correct information when thrown.

In actual fact, divining by means of dice is not confined to nganga; ordinary people may practice such divination as well. However, since nganga are recognised as the chosen ones in whom spiritual power resides, they are understandably able to provide the final, most expert diagnosis.

Some diviners do not rely upon dice for diagnostic answers or guidance, but depend entirely upon ritual possession by their particular spirit. Such nganga require helpers to assist them in collecting fees and inducing the spirit to enter its host. This may be done by the assistant's clapping of hands or of giving the nganga snuff to inhale. The spirit usually speaks in a different voice from the nganga's, and the person desiring help can address the spirit voice and get a direct reply.

Ideally, before a diagnosis is made, clients share every detail about their family life, their fears, their enemies, etc with the nganga. The nganga thus performs a function similar to that of a psychotherapist in Western societies. Tension in a community is often the source of individual's troubles and has to be dealt with before healing can take place.

Very often the nganga finds that some obligation has been neglected, such as unperformed rituals, slighting an ancestor or withholding help from the living community. Another common cause of serious trouble is witchcraft. Once the source of the trouble has been ascertained appropriate steps must be taken.

Where a ritual has been overlooked, it must be performed; if living members of the family have been neglected, they must be cared for. Wrongs must be set right.

In addition, a nganga may give medicine to treat the immediate symptoms of the trouble. Many ngangas specialise in either herbalism or divination, although often one nganga performs both functions. Some ngangas are well-known for their ability to treat a particular type of illness, as certain remedies are passed down from generation to generation.

If the cause of the trouble is diagnosed as witchcraft (*uroyi*) the remedy is not easily found. Although most ancestral spirits are benevolent, there are those that seek to bring evil upon the community. They too seek a host among members of their living family. These evil spirits are called *muroyi* (plural: *varoyi*) and, like the harmful ngozi spirits, are greatly feared.

Evil and harm may at times be concentrated in a human individual, usually a female. Such a person is known as a *muroyi wedzinza* or hereditary witch, who inherits her craft from a maternal ancestor. In this class of witches, as in other forms of spirit possession, the harmful spirit seeks to make itself known. Thus, although spirit possession is widespread in Shona communities and generally interpreted positively, not all possession is welcomed.

Since there are degrees of evil, the damage which may be inflicted varies from muroyi to muroyi. Some general ideas concerning witches are that they go about naked at night when they meet in cultic collusion. They are accused of visiting the graves of dead people, of eating human flesh (especially that of a child) and of making medicine from human flesh and bodily parts. In addition they may ride a hyena or own an owl - creatures known as 'witch familiars'.

Although the evil epitomised by witchcraft may attack at random, it is more often related to tension which develops in a family or community setting. At such times those who are known to have convicted witches among their ancestry and who, in one way or another, have exhibited antisocial behaviour are likely to be suspected. Since it is believed that a witch can do evil unwittingly, the accused are often unsure of themselves and may confess to being a witch in the hope of being restored to the community through exorcism.

Not all witches, however, belong to this class. People may also become witches through their own desire to harm or seek vengeance on others. In addition to the muroyi who works at night and is habitually evil, there is also another class of witches characterised as the *muroyi wamasikati*, a daytime witch or sorcerer who, more often than not, is male. This type of witchcraft or sorcery is occasional and not intrinsic to the psychic personality of the individual. Thus any person who uses medicine which has a harmful effect on someone else, even though it may be designed to protect the user, may be considered to be a muroyi (Daneel 1971:160-162). For example, person A may suspect that person B in the community is planning to do him harm. In consultation with a nganga, person A retaliates by placing medicine that causes evil in person B's way. Person B becomes ill and person A is liable to be accused of being a muroyi wamasikati.

It is readily apparent that ngangas are integral to this whole complex of good and evil, not only because of their contact with the power of the spirit world, but also because they are the dispensers of medicines which may either harm or heal, depending on the perspective from which the situation is viewed. As indicated above, medicine designed to protect one individual may do so by having a harmful effect on another. Furthermore it must be recognised that some ngangas do, in fact, become corrupt and act as varoyi. Nevertheless, the accepted role of the nganga is that of a benefactor of the community, while the usual role of the muroyi is that of a harmful, socially detrimental person.

The word 'muroyi' may be used in a wider context as well, but however it is used, it always implies antisocial, unacceptable actions that are harmful to the community. Open accusations of witchcraft are always preceded by tension and conflict in the community concerned. With this in mind we turn now to the Shona belief in the continuing community.

Belief in the continuing community

If a geometrical shape were chosen to symbolise Shona life and culture, it might be a circular form with concentric circles moving from the core outward. Let the inner circle stand for the tightly woven relationships which enable each individual to realise his or her own personhood. The phrase 'I am because I belong' is basic to the essence of religious experience throughout Africa. It can be said that Africa's religiosity gives expression to this in African life. This is particularly apposite in the case of the Shona people. Social and religious relationships form the warp and weft of Shona life, so that one cannot, in fact, discuss their religion without acknowledging Shona cultural activities as expressed in and through society.

The concentric circles which extend outward from the inner, personal circle would represent the genealogical relationships which support and tie an individual, first to the family unit, then to the extended family or village, and finally to the clan. These ritualised relationships also include those ancesto on in the memory of their loved ones, while the rituals, by their ver protect those not yet born into the community.

At the core of the circle, then, is the individual who realises his or her personhood as a member of a gradually expanding group of ever widening relationships within the nyika. Beliefs and practices which strengthen these lineage relationships, especially those surrounding marriage and death, are of extreme importance. In both these events the person is passing into a new existence - that of a married, contributing adult and that of a practising, invisible ancestor.

Marriage customs

When a boy and girl of marriageable age are attracted to one another the following procedure is customary. Marriage is a lengthy, drawn-out business rather than a single official occasion. At the outset love tokens are exchanged, whereby the boy and the girl let each other know that they would be willing for marriage arrangements to be initiated. After this private acknowledgment, the two families are brought into the matter. Among the Manyika people the *vatete* (paternal aunts) of both the boy's and the girl's families open the negotiations. They must first assure that the totemic praise names of the young couple differ before the question of bridewealth can be discussed.

Bridewealth (usually an agreed number of cattle or, nowadays, cash) is paid to the girl's father. Although the young man is responsible for paying it, it is understood that his family will support and help him, since they all stand to benefit from the addition of a young woman to their group. The payment of cattle has symbolic religious significance in that cattle represent the continuing prosperity of the community.

During this time a series of ritualised meetings takes place. It starts with the sending of an intermediary from the boy's village to the girl's village with a symbolic gift, sometimes a hoe. As arrangements proceed, each step of acceptance is marked by the families sitting down together to a communal meal.

Bridewealth may be understood as a guarantee of good faith on the part of both families. The payment makes it difficult for either party to break the marriage arrangement at a later date. The wife realises that if she decides to return to her father's village, he must repay most of the bridewealth. If the husband later becomes dissatisfied with his wife and sends her back to her home, he knows that he will forfeit the cattle or money which he has paid. Bridewealth, then, is a gift symbolising an earnest belief in the successful outcome of the proposed marriage.

In addition to the agreed amount of bridewealth, it is generally expected that a gift of appreciation (usually a cow) will be given to the bride's mother.

After a certain amount of the agreed bridewealth has been paid, the girl's father allows the groom to sleep with his bride and eventually to take her to his homestead. She must, however, return to her parental home for the birth of her first child, when a further portion of the bridewealth will be paid before the new mother and child return with her husband to his homestead.

According to Shona custom a man may have more than one wife. A situation which precipitates such an arrangement is the death of a man's brother. The living brother is expected to take over the wife or wives of his dead brother. As might be expected, jealousies often occur between wives as well as between the children of different wives. However, the resulting emotional trauma is probably no worse than that caused by remarriage after divorce in Western homes. Adultery is probably less common in African communities than in Western ones. Although there are provisions for divorce amongst the Shona, it is not common due to the restraint placed on the couple by the bridewealth (Gelfand 1981:18-20).

Children are always a welcome addition to any homestead and in cases of barrenness the nganga is consulted to learn the reason. It may be a manifestation of ancestral disapproval which needs to be dealt with. It may indicate the presence of unwelcome ngozi spirits which have to be exorcised, or witchcraft may be suspected.

Among the Shona in general it is expected that each person's life will move normally through the anticipated stages preceding death. Just as marriage is a gradual affair, so is death.

Death customs

As a person moves beyond the age of producing children, he or she is treated with increasing respect. Age, in Shona culture, does not mean isolation from the activities of the household but rather that the person functions in an advisory rather than a physically contributory capacity.

When an older member of the community dies, there are certain ritualised procedures to be followed. Although the details of these procedures vary greatly among Shona groups, a more or less general pattern emerges whereby the deceased becomes an ancestor (mudzimu) or spirit elder - the most senior member of the community who has become a spirit.

Upon the death of a person, relatives and friends are all informed before the body is washed and prepared for burial. Traditionally the corpse is then wrapped in a new blanket and placed on a mat. Relatives and friends come to pay their final respects by means of a small gift (perhaps a coin) and respectful clapping of hands.

A funerary procession then proceeds to the newly dug grave, usually within twenty-four hours of death. The sons-in-law of the deceased carry the body, stopping from time to time. This is to allow the spirit of the dead person to rest and to turn the body frequently, so that whereas the deceased left the homestead feet first, he or she arrives at the burial spot head first. After the body has been lowered into the grave all present join in throwing a handful of soil into the grave. Then they return to the homestead where a meal of meat and firm porridge has been prepared by the daughters-in-law. A purification ritual must be observed by those who participated in the funeral before they can partake of the meal (Gelfand 1977:96-101).

A diviner is often consulted concerning the cause of death, especially if it did not appear to be a natural consequence of old age.

A further ceremony is held, usually two to three months after the burial of the deceased, in which the spirit of the dead person is 'cooled' symbolically. This ritual is intended to deal with the inevitable tensions arising from any change in social status, including the death of an individual. An inheritance ceremony may be performed as part of this occasion, or it may be postponed till the more important final ceremony (*kugadzira* or *kurowa guwa*) which occurs about a year after the death. This ceremony is held to settle the spirit and to elevate it ritually to ancestral status.

The inheritance ceremony is usually held only for a male who has produced offspring. At this ceremony his wife/wives, as well as his name and position in the community, are among the possessions which are inherited by the appropriately designated members of the homestead.

Since the living and the dead form part of the continuing community for the Shona, the final ceremony whereby the deceased joins the realm of protective ancestors and returns to assume guardianship of the homestead, is of vital importance. The sharing of a communal meal, which includes ritually brewed beer, is an important part of this ceremony. All members of the family are expected to share the cost of the meal and to partake of the food and beer. Sometimes the ancestral spirit is symbolically returned to the home in the form of a ceremonially prepared goat. At this time family relationships are reaffirmed, the deceased person retaining his proper position in the kinship structure. Thereafter the person is remembered in community ceremonies from time to time, along with other spirit elders of the group.

Although this chapter gives only a very brief review of Shona religious practices, it suggests the overall view of life which characterises Shona culture. It emerges that for the Shona the ideal life is group-oriented with a spiritual, albeit anthropomorphic, dimension. In contrast to the Western approach, the Shona life view is less segmented and less individualistic.

SUGGESTED READING

Daneel, M L 1970. *The god of the Matopo Hills: an essay on the Mwari cult in Rhodesia.* The Hague: Mouton.

Daneel, M L 1974. *Old and new in southern Shona independent churches.* Volume I: Background and rise of the movement. The Hague: Mouton.

Bourdillon, M F C 1976. *The Shona peoples.* Gwelo: Mambo Press.

Gelfand, M 1981. *Ukama: reflections on Shona and Western cultures in Zimbabwe.* Gwelo: Mambo Press.

CHAPTER 5

The Mbuti pygmies

In spite of an apparent lack of structured ritual and worship the Mbuti pygmies have a profound sense of the sacred which permeates all of their daily activities. This chapter gives a review of their religious orientation to life by way of an outline of their cultural activities.

HISTORICAL AND CULTURAL REVIEW

Often that which is written (or spoken) tells more about the writer (speaker) than about the subject under discussion. An illustration of this is found in the early written accounts of the pygmies of the Central African rain forests. Over 4 000 years ago an ancient Egyptian, a high official at the court of Pharaoh Pepi II Neferkere (2275-2185 BCE), described a people living in the rain forests of Africa who were singers and dancers and who displayed a religious devotion to the forest itself. His report mentions only incidentally that they were short in stature. No doubt the Egyptian official's description of the pygmy people would accord with their own perception of themselves.

In marked contrast were the depictions by a fourteenth century cartographer who portrayed the pygmies as semi-monsters or anthropoid apes (troglodytes). Myths persisted, both before and after this description by the cartographer of the Hereford Mappa Mundi. There was also one refreshing sixth century review whose author perceived them to be real people. By and large, however, sensational stories always spread more readily than factual accounts, and the pygmies were variously described as being able to fly from treetop to treetop, as having tails and as crawling on their bellies like snakes.

Eventually, in the seventeenth century (just prior to the 'age of reason') an English anatomist decided that such ridiculous fabrications needed to be squelched. After carefully examining a skeleton believed to be that of a pygmy, he pronounced that it was in fact that of a chimpanzee and without further ado declared the existence of the entire pygmy population to be merely a fable.

Not until the nineteenth century was the presence of real people living in the Ituri rain forest reconfirmed by explorers. Interest in these mysterious small people thereafter attracted anthropological attention. Nevertheless the available literature on the pygmies of the Ituri rain forest remains limited to this day.

The first point concerning these near mythical, mysterious people is that they have inhabited the area for a very long time, most likely for at least 5 000 years. This figure must remain an estimate, however, as a rain forest does not lend itself to archaeological investigation as material evidence is quickly destroyed.

In spite of the lack of material evidence, some logical conclusions can be drawn. If, as the earliest records aver, these people had an affinity with the forest, their life style has probably changed relatively little since those times, for they must of necessity have maintained an optimal level of adaptation to their environment over the centuries. During the period under consideration there have been no known cataclysmic changes in this area such as might have forced the forest dwellers to adapt their life style in any radical way.

It is interesting that wall paintings have been discovered at Pompeii (c 500 BCE) which depict pygmies living in beehive-shaped dwellings, strikingly similar in appearance to those used by the Ituri forest people today.

Any direct relationship between the pygmies, whose adult height is approximately 1,35 meters, and their slightly larger San neighbours to the south has not been positively established. It seems not unlikely that such a relationship might exist.

In addition to their short stature, pygmies have other distinguishing features. Their legs are generally short in proportion to their bodies, which gives them a muscular appearance. Their round faces have wide-set eyes and flat noses almost as broad as their mouths are wide. The hair on their heads grows in tight peppercorn tufts and, while some pygmies have little or no body hair, others have an abundance. According to Turnbull (1961:33), whose books were a major source for the material presented in this chapter, they always create an impression of alertness, both in their facial expressions and in their bodily movements, which are marked by speed and agility.

There are ten or more different populations of these small people inhabiting the tropical rain forest which forms part of seven present-day African countries: Burundi, Cameroon, the Central African Republic, Gabon, the People's Republic of the Congo, Rwanda and Zaire. Although these pygmy groups are not necessarily related to one another, they have all responded similarly to the forest and to their Bantu and Sudanese neighbours who live on the fringes of the forest.

The descriptive word 'pygmy' comes from the Greek, *pygme*, a unit of measurement designating the length from the elbow to the knuckles (Bailey 1989:669). Obviously the people do not refer to themselves as pygmies but use their local tribal names, such as Epulu or Efe. Living a semi-nomadic life primarily in the forest areas, but increasingly today in interaction with their agriculturist Sudanese or Bantu neighbours, their population is estimated at 150 000 to 200 000 (Bailey 1989:669). Perhaps they are best described as children of the forest, where their small stature is a distinct advantage.

The Ituri rain forest in the geographical centre of the African continent gives the impression of being both limitless and part of another world. Its vastness is conveyed by its diameter, which is hundreds of miles, and by its height. Huge trees tower as high as 54 meters or more into the air, their broad leaves forming a roof-like canopy shutting out the direct rays of the sun. For the Mbuti the forest represents the protective, cool shelter of home. It is the haven to which they retreat again and again for nourishment and revitalisation. These children of the forest are naturally adapted to their environment, since bigger is not better in the humid heat of a rain forest.

There the Mbuti and other pygmy groups maintain what may be described as a pre-stone-age culture: they do not have stone implements and only in recent times have they begun to make use of the iron made available to them by immigrant populations. Nevertheless they have learned to utilise their forest world to its highest potential by means of socially cooperative ventures.

One of the clearest examples is the way in which the Mbuti hunt. Although, generally speaking, the men are hunters and the women gatherers of edible fruits, roots and bulbs, in actual practice both men and women and even older children are involved in a hunt.

The first step is for the men to prepare their nets. This is a joint effort in which they all help to uncoil the lengths of knotted twine which may measure as much as 90 meters. Two men work together, one holding the net off the ground while the other inspects it for tears and then coils it again in such a way that it hangs from his shoulder to just above his ankles. The net is then tied with a loose piece of twine and hung on a tree branch, ready for use. Each man is responsible for having his net in good working order so that the eventual hunt, which is a team effort, will not be thwarted. This can only be done if everyone cooperates from start to finish.

Often there is a dance in the camp before everyone leaves to join in the hunt. Both men and women form a circle, singing a hunting song and clapping their hands. They look about carefully as if trying to spot game while they make exaggerated leaps into the air in imitation of the animals they hope to catch. One necessary ritual act before a hunt can commence is the lighting of a sacred fire. Some groups choose a site at the base of a tree a short distance from the camp, while others light it within the camp. Among the Mbuti these ritualised actions are carried out so casually that they may not even be noticed by an outsider. The children take burning sticks from a fire that they have previously lit in their *bopi* (play area) with embers from their individual family hearths. They set off in the direction which the day's hunt is to take and when they find the right tree they light the fire at its base, covering it with special leaves so that it gives off huge columns of smoke. All those who are about to participate in the hunt must file past this fire. Some of the hunters stop and let the smoke engulf them, while others may reach into the smoke and rub it on their bodies with their hands as if washing themselves in it. The Mbuti regard fire as a most precious gift and in this way they acknowledge their debt to and dependence upon the forest (Turnbull 1961:98).

As the women move along the path to join in the hunt, they gather food - nuts, mushrooms, berries, sweet roots. These actually form the bulk of the daily diet and add variety and flavour to the meat from the hunt when it is eventually cooked.

Once they have arrived at the spot chosen for the day's hunt, the men set up their nets in a semicircle, one after the other, leaving no gaps in between. The nets are fastened to the ground below and to the branches of the trees above. By this time the women have quietly taken up position beyond the nets. At a given signal they begin to beat the ground, shouting and generally making a great deal of noise. This frightens the animals in the area so that they run into the nets where the men can stab them to death or even kill them with their bare hands.

Occasionally larger animals such as leopards, buffalo, even elephants, turn round to face the advancing women and youths. The women may cry out a warning to the men if large game is sighted, so that they can lower the nets and let the animal pass without tearing the nets or injuring the people who are giving chase. Male youths are positioned at both ends of the nets, sometimes armed with spears or bows and arrows, so that they can catch any animal which attempts to escape around the side. This is the opportunity for the youths to prove themselves as hunters, sometimes by killing the animal with their bare hands. Thus they prove that they are ready for marriage arrangements to be made.

The slaughtered animal is usually taken back to camp where it is divided into portions, choice pieces going to the one whose spear struck the death blow. However, since the entire hunt is a cooperative enterprise, no one goes hungry. Small deer are the animals most commonly caught by the Mbuti net-hunters.

As soon as the hunters return with the meat, the camp comes to life. Everyone gathers around to be sure that the meat is divided fairly. In spite of much controversy about the matter, in the end everyone is satisfied. The women go off to cook the meat that has been divided into family-sized portions, adding flavour and variety by means of mushrooms, forest herbs or sweet *itaba* roots. After all have eaten, the Mbuti may conclude the day's activities with more dancing and storytelling, often centring on the day's activities.

Other groups of Ituri forest pygmies hunt in slightly differing ways. The Efe, at the northeastern tip of the Zaire river basin, for example, hunt with bows and arrows with poisoned tips. Monkeys are their most common source of meat. Among these groups too the hunt is always a cooperative undertaking.

Although there is no real division of labour, it is usually the women who carry what belongings the family may have when it is time to move camp. The packs may weigh as much as eighteen kilograms, approximately half their body weight. The men maintain that not only are women stronger than they are, but that they must have their hands free in case they come upon game unexpectedly. In addition every woman carries a burning ember wrapped in fire-resistant leaves. Whenever the group pauses to rest on the trail, the first action is to unwrap the ember and light a fire by arranging sticks around it and blowing softly. Since the forest is damp and cool such a fire is always welcome, even in the daytime, but more so at night when it offers protection from wild animals.

It is also the women's responsibility to care for the huts in which the family units sleep. These low, beehive-shaped dwellings are made from a framework of saplings and twigs over which large *mongonga* leaves are placed like tiles, the upper row overlapping the lower. These large heart-shaped leaves may be up to 60 centimetres wide. The huts need to be tidied daily and new leaves added or old ones rearranged to prevent the frequent rains from leaking into the huts. Entrances to the huts may easily be shifted depending upon whim or circumstance. Likewise the hut may be enlarged to accommodate visiting relatives from neighbouring camps.

Pygmies change camp locations in the forest more or less on a monthly basis, although they stay within certain recognised territorial hunting limits within the forest.

As children of the forest pygmies have a working relationship with the Bantu or Sudanese agriculturists who inhabit the areas bordering on the Ituri forest. From time to time the pygmies emerge from the forest to visit the village-dwellers to whom they 'belong'. They may bring with them meat or honey, which is greatly appreciated by the agriculturists. This they exchange for vegetables or manufactured goods, such as cooking pots or items of clothing. They take great pleasure in tricking the villagers by feigning an attitude of subservience.

Frequently they live for brief periods in settlements attached to the adjoining African villages. During these times, the villagers rely on help from the pygmies for the planting or harvesting of their crops. A symbiotic relationship exists between particular villagers and certain pygmy groups, whom the agriculturists refer to as 'our pygmies'. They often attempt to 'convert' their pygmies to village ways, including their cultural and religious conceptions. Each pygmy has two names, one in his own Mbuti language and one in his Bantu or Sudanese village language. The pygmies, who willingly submit to their seemingly servile situation, remain in or near the village as long as there is anything to be gained. Then, as quickly and quietly as they came, they depart again to the comforting haunts of their forest sanctuary.

Pygmy camps are usually at least an hour's walk from the nearest village. If the pygmies want to remain relatively nearby for raiding purposes, they do so; otherwise they retreat deeper into the heart of the forest. They are well aware that they are safe from pursuit by the villagers, who do not dare venture far into the mysterious, to them forbidden depths of the forest, not even to retrieve stolen goods.

The following description of a day in the life of a pygmy camp is adapted from Dupré (1975:154-155).

Rising time is determined by the weather. If the sun is shining, life in the camp - which comprises four to twelve huts - begins early. If it is cloudy or raining, the people move about in a more leisurely and lethargic manner. In either case, the women take their children and go in search of bulbs, roots, mushrooms or fruits. They sing as they go about their work. Before they begin they ask for help in finding desired items of food. Their requests may be addressed to *tore*, *epilipili* or *mungu*. (These names are not consistent - pygmy groups may use different names in their prayers and rituals. Neither are the names confined to one group only: they recur throughout the region, although certain names may be prevalent in certain areas.) When they discover newly ripened fruits, a symbolic portion is set aside. At the end of the search, when the work of cooking and the eating are done, small pieces of food are laid aside on a leaf. This is all part of the preparation for the next day's labours - part of the continuing cycle of life in the forest.

While the women concern themselves with the gathering of food, the men are preparing for the hunt. They, too, call upon tore, epilipili or mungu, or even on their departed fathers, to further their success. When an animal has been killed and brought into the camp to be divided among the families, the eldest member supervises. This is understood to be according to a law established first by tore. At the same time a specified piece of the animal (the heart or some other organ) is thrown back into the forest or put aside on a leaf laid either on the ground or in the fork of a tree. This would seem to be an expression of basic gratitude to mungu (or the forest), and it is maintained that only stupid people fail to carry out this ritual.

At night the hunter, having uttered an invocation, places his spear beside the place where he has left the meat offering in preparation for the next day's work. He may receive instructions for the next day in his dreams, particularly if he places an arrow beneath his head. These instructions may concern a successful hunt or the proper time for moving camp. Usually it is the eldest member of the group who receives such instructions.

If a hunter finds other desirable edibles in the course of his work, such as a honey tree or termites, a sacramental portion is laid aside in gratitude. If the hunt is a particularly dangerous one, such as a search for elephants, the wives may perform a type of libation ceremony in which they fill their mouths with water and squirt it over their husbands. They then ask for help and protection for the men.

> Considering the overall picture of a typical pygmy day, we can say that man's work and behaviour begins with and ends in absolute symbolism. Even in the most primitive ... pygmy culture, where the fulfillment of essential needs exhausts almost all time available, man is highly aware of something that expresses clearly that there is no human act for its own sake.
>
> (Dupré 1975:154/5)

The pygmies' daily symbolic actions seem to indicate awareness of a meaning beyond what is visibly or rationally determined. It would be unjustified, however, to describe these actions as irrational, since they do not interfere with rational behaviour. This leads to the conclusion that these actions are part of what may be called the religious dimension of their lives. We therefore proceed to analyse those aspects of pygmy behaviour which seem to have religious content, under the following topics: societal ethics, concept of God, rituals and symbols.

THE RELIGIOUS ORIENTATION OF THE MBUTI

It would be incorrect to state that the Mbuti have precisely delineated theories or doctrines either about God or about man and his place in the universe. Nevertheless an analysis of Mbuti behaviour indicates that the Mbuti do, indeed, have concepts of religious significance. Since their socio-ethical code is the most readily observable, a discussion of religious conceptions naturally begins at this point.

Socio-ethical relationships

The basic social unit among the Mbuti is the hunting band or camp. This group recognises itself as a family and members refer to one another in kinship terms. However, the band changes frequently, in respect of both location and composition. The only factors limiting the composition of a group are the need for mobility (it must not become too large) and a linguistic factor - there are a considerable number of linguistic variations among the pygmies. At times the fusion and fission process of individuals splitting off from one group to join another is so rapid as to make it quite impossible to identify extended family units beyond the parent-child relationship. The importance of this parent-child relationship for the group is evident from a number of things.

Lineage does not receive undue attention among the Mbuti. Instead the group is strengthened by the knowledge that each was wanted as a child. There is virtually no differentiation between males and females during childhood and old age. It is only in the child-bearing years that a difference is recognised. Although sex outside marriage is not forbidden as long as privacy and respect for others are observed, it is understood that partners in these liaisons do not 'fully embrace' but hold one another 'by the elbows'. It is further maintained that children are never born out of wedlock. Turnbull (1983:34) indicates that he could find no record of this ever having occurred, although he could offer no plausible explanation apart from the possible use of some unknown herbal contraceptive.

The important point is that people only marry because they want to have children and all Mbuti know that they were born because they were wanted. This knowledge not only gives the individual security, but extends to the relationship within the hunting band/camp, which is composed of people who are together because they desire to be so. Within the family camp, then, there are no such categories as childless women, orphans or lonely old people. All members of the group belong to one another.

Although the Mbuti may submit to Bantu marriage rituals during periodic visits to their villages, real marriages occur within their forest home. Such a marriage involves an exchange of visits between the families concerned and the presentation of a gift (usually a large antelope or a bow and arrows) by the groom to the bride's family. It is expected, in addition, that the groom will supply a female marriage partner for someone in the bride's camp. This may be a sister or other near relative. A balance is thus maintained, since the women normally see to such household tasks as cooking and care of the huts. It is clear, then, that a woman is considered an essential partner in Mbuti society. A group that loses a woman seeks another to replace her. Since the term 'brother' or 'sister' is extended to almost anyone in the same age group, it is usually possible to find some relative, however distant, who qualifies.

One difficulty in such a sister-exchange situation, however, is that if one marriage disintegrates, the corresponding marriage is expected to break up as well, both women returning to their original families.

Once preliminary arrangements have been agreed upon, the bride simply moves into the groom's hut and begins to prepare his food. The camp awaits the arrival of their first child.

Mother and father share in caring for a newborn baby. The infant is wrapped in a piece of decorated bark cloth freshly cut from a tree. Thus the child's first protection outside the womb comes from the forest.

A baby is breast-fed for the first three years of its life. In the second year, however, it is the father who introduces the child to its first solid food. This is done during a meaningful ceremony which is held in the centre of the camp, where all important, binding statements are made. The mother hands the child to the father who holds it close to his chest. When the child attempts to suckle and cries *ema* (mother), the father holds it away from him, saying, *eba* (father). He then gives it its first solid food.

At the age of three the child is permitted to join other children in the play area called the bopi. In this smaller area, about ninety metres from the main camp, the children reign supreme. Immediately upon entrance they are made aware of the importance of age as a structural standard of authority. Later, through games, they learn the skills that will enable them eventually to join in adult cooperative ventures that ensure the economic survival of the group in the forest. If adults attempt to enter the bopi in anger - for example, when their rest has been disturbed - the children drive them away with taunts and jeers. It is clear that Mbuti regard children as people who, like adults, have both privileges and responsibilities.

One task that is reserved exclusively for children is the lighting of the sacred fire for the initiation of the daily hunt. Only children who have not yet been contaminated by the 'sin' of killing animals for food are pure enough to light that fire, which symbolises the pygmies' identity with their forest world. If the fire is not lit by children, the hunt cannot take place. As soon as older children or youths join in the hunt, even on the sidelines at the ends of the nets, they are no longer eligible for the daily fire-lighting.

Youths, however, have their own special area of responsibility, which is to act as the lawmakers and judges of the group. Strange as it may seem, young people, who have not yet encountered the deep emotional conflicts caused by marital or other associations, are considered ideal for this task. Furthermore, their singing and dancing abilities are at their peak during these years, and it is by means of song and dance that conflicts are usually resolved (Turnbull 1983:50).

For the Mbuti the ideal situation is one of harmony and peace. Individual justice is upheld only inasmuch as it contributes to the well-being of the group, which, in turn, has to live in holistic unity with its forest environment. The word *akami*, which can be translated as 'noise', has little to do with the decibel level of sound, and everything to do with its cause. Happy chatter and banter are signs of *ekimi* (the opposite of akami), as are silence or song and dance. Ekimi is welcome, being evidence of holistic cooperation, while akami is feared and hated. Humour is often used effectively by the Mbuti to allay or avoid serious disputes which might result in akami.

The daily workload of hunting, gathering and preparing food falls upon the adult members, among whom there is surprisingly little differentiation between tasks for men and women. The responsibility for making authoritative decisions rests with the elder members of the camp. Although belief in ancestral intervention is not nearly as strong as among Bantu people, the affirmation, 'my father told me so', is a validating principle underlying many customs. The authority of the elder, however, depends upon the cooperation of the group: if it is felt that he has acted out of self-interest rather than in the interests of the group his decision may be disregarded. He is simply *primus inter pares* in a group where unity is of utmost importance.

Although there are legends indicating that pygmies simply abandon old people who can no longer contribute to the well-being of the group, neither Turnbull nor Schebesta found any evidence to support these stories. Turnbull (1961:47-51) in fact witnessed the death and burial of an old mother of the group. After her body had been placed in the ground, it was suggested that the best way to preserve her memory and to regain their own sense of well-being would be to return to the forest, since the old woman had died while the Mbuti were temporarily residing near their Bantu village. This return was promptly effected.

Schebesta (Dupré 1975:156) questioned the groups of Mbuti among whom he did fieldwork concerning their beliefs in life after death. At first he was told that there is nothing beyond the present life. Death is the end. However, upon further observation and discussion, he gathered that a person is understood to consist of more than merely a body. In terms of bodily existence alone, death is final. But a person is also his *tedi* or shadow and *borupi*, a word which is difficult to translate but which seems to refer to the heart or eyes and to fire. Possibly it indicates the seat of human emotions and feeling. Borupi is the spark which keeps the heart beating and the life reflected in a person's eyes. When breath ceases, borupi unites with tore. There are various interpretations of where or what tore may be, but it is conceptualised as both the forest and the sky.

At least some groups of pygmies believe that a dead person turns into his *giniso* or totem at death. The totem is usually an animal (leopard, chimpanzee, buffalo), a reptile or a bird. It is taboo to eat or to kill one's own totem, as this may spell illness or death for the entire group. Everyone has a totem and if a woman's totem differs from her husband's, she has to respect his totem, at least in his presence.

Dreams are the principal means of communication between the living and the dead. It is understood that the living are with the dead or with tore when they are dreaming about their respective totems. The giniso or totem is considered to be the residue of the dream world which remains when a person awakens. It is, in a sense, the abstract presence of the ancestor, megbe, or tore which exists in the physical world. The giniso may be addressed as 'father' (ancestor) and may be called upon for help in hunting.

In addition to totem taboos, there are also taboos on other animals, birds and plants. Among these, the taboos concerning the chameleon are the most stringent. The chameleon is said to be a very old animal and it is necessary to spit in its direction (sputum represents one's vital force) if one comes upon it unexpectedly in the forest. Among some groups of Mbuti there is a myth to the effect that the chameleon opened the forest and set mankind free from the interior of a primal mythic tree. Thus the chameleon symbolises the creative power (megbe) of the moon/forest - a symbolism extended to certain other taboo objects, including the giniso.

The term megbe used above relates to those concepts of divinity which persist among the Mbuti.

Conceptions of divinity

Although the various pygmy groups entertain a relatively wide spectrum of beliefs concerning the forest, the moon, the chameleon, etc, one basic principle seems to obtain more or less universally, albeit expressed by different names. This principle is designated here by the term, megbe, which could be translated as vital or living force. Megbe is considered to be the ground from which people emerge and by which they live. It gives them power to act, to speak and to think - to be, in effect, a vital human being. When megbe fades and leaves the body, breath ceases and the person no longer exists as a human being.

A person's megbe does not cease to exist with death, however. It returns to the moon or the forest. Every person possesses megbe by virtue of being born. The oldest and most successful hunters and wise people are believed to have an abundance of megbe. When the hunter calls upon his totem or his father to ensure a good hunt, he is at the same time trusting in his megbe. The elder of the clan likewise relies on megbe when he makes decisions which affect the group. Without this force, nothing endures or succeeds. As mentioned, it is imperishable and, although it returns to the moon or forest when an individual dies, it re-enters the world at the birth of each child. It is, in essence, that divine principle whereby the polar end of life becomes a new beginning. Life is lived according to this mythic dimension which constitutes the continuity of all things.

Megbe is the visible manifestation of the invisible creative power residing in the forest or the moon. Although the names for this original creative force differ from place to place, the underlying concept seems to be common to all Mbuti tribes. The following is a summary of some of the related ideas, based on Dupré's (1975:171-177) interpretation of Schebesta's findings.

The Forest owns the forest and the life in it. On the one hand he is a father or a grandfather; on the other hand he may be an evil force, punishing humans by death through the glance of his eyes and the lightning flash. Both successful and futile hunts are attributed to his will. He is almighty. Everything was made by him, including animals which are his property. He sees everything, and people are socially, and therefore ethically, responsible to him. He communicates with mankind in dreams or by means of less spectacular manifestations, such as a slap on the upper arm.

The Moon too is the ruler of all human and divine beings. He created people and the world and continues to create through menstrual blood (known also as elima or megbe). He forms the child in the womb and places a limit on its lifespan. He is the source and recipient of a person's borupi. As with the Forest, the visible and the mythical moon are differentiated by saying that the moon was created by the Moon. Both the chameleon and the rainbow are symbols of the Moon. The chameleon lives in the tree tops because there it is closest to the moon, and its throaty cry is known as the voice of the Forest God. The Moon has the same ambivalent character as the Forest, in that his symbol - the rainbow - is considered to be benevolent if it is in the west, but inauspicious if in the east.

The words *tore, epilipili, mungu* and others are used by different groups to refer to both the Moon and the Forest. If they in fact represent creative, eternal power, is this so very far removed from the basic concept of God found among other world religions? Although the Mbuti lack the structured theology of a religious system, the basic religious intuitions upon which such systems are built seem to be decidedly present. Other basic religious conceptions are found in Mbuti mythology, which reveals a permanent quest for the beginning - the origin of humankind and all things - and, at the same time, provides an absolute explanation of the world as it is. Here are two myths, both greatly abridged.

In the beginning the moon left the earth and went to heaven, but his representative, the chameleon, remained behind. While the chameleon was strolling through the forest he heard a rustling noise in a certain tree. By means of his hatchet (the crescent moon) he opened the tree and water flowed out, gushing forth over the earth. The water combined with blood, and so a son, the ancestor of all humankind, was born.

Mungu made the first man and told him he would be the father of many children who would live and be happy in the forest. But he also stipulated that the fruit of the *tahu* tree was taboo and should not be eaten. One day, while the first man went to the sky on a visit, a pregnant woman desired the fruit of the *tahu* tree. Her husband finally gave in to her demands, picked it and gave her a piece of the forbidden fruit. The Moon witnessed this transgression and told Mungu, who sent death as a punishment.

The Mbuti, who have a bare minimum of cultural objects, nevertheless value such implements as they possess. The existence of these items is attributed to a 'culture hero' or a 'bringer of blessings' called, *Aparofandza*. It is said that he had many, many children to whom he gave the necessary tools to make a livelihood and taught them everything they needed to know, especially the use of the bow and arrow and the method of procreation.

The Mbuti's reverence for the forest is also reflected in their festivals and rituals.

Religious rituals

Probably the most salient feature of religious ritual among the Mbuti is its near absence. Actions of ritual significance are performed so naturally and unobtrusively that they are likely to go undetected, even by a trained anthropologist. Several of these symbolic acts have already been mentioned, particularly in the description of a typical pygmy day. At least two other ritual activities deserve attention: the *molimo* festival and the *elima* celebration.

A *molimo* festival requires the group's presence in the forest. Once the camp site has been chosen and the huts have been built, two youths go from dwelling to dwelling with a basket and a length of cord, made from the same vines as are used to make hunting nets. They make a noose at one end of the cord and place it before the entrance to each hut. The woman of the home is expected to place a food offering in this noose, whereupon one of the youths tugs it away and transfers the food thus obtained to the basket held by the other young man. Finally, when food has been collected from every hut, the full basket is hung on a branch next to the communal fire, built from burning logs that were collected from each nuclear family hearth. This fire is called the kumamolimo (place of the molimo) and the food that has been collected is for the molimo, who is said to be a 'hungry animal'.

The molimo trumpet is one sacred object collectively owned by a pygmy group. Turnbull (1961:73-93), who was privileged to participate in a molimo festival, was shocked by his initial sight of the trumpet. He saw to his amazement that it was no more than an old, slightly bent piece of drain pipe that had, in all likelihood, been stolen from a road-construction gang. He was made to understand that although traditionally the pipes were fashioned from bamboo, it did not matter what their material substance was, as long as they 'worked'. A metal pipe was more practical than wood because it would not rot. By night the pipe-trumpet, approximately 4,6 meters in length, was carefully and secretly carried through the forest to the pygmy camp. Children and women were forbidden to see the molimo trumpet and its use and care were committed exclusively to the young men of the camp.

As they travelled on foot through the forest, the young men paused at each stream to wash and 'feed' the trumpet with water. In the case of a wooden trumpet this procedure would have had practical value, since it would cause the wood to swell and cracks to close, thus improving the sound of the instrument. In the case of a metal pipe the procedure had only ritual value.

As they approached the village, the youths began to blow into the trumpet one after another, reproducing the sounds of the forest so exactly that it seemed to Turnbull as if the night had suddenly come alive with the rumblings and growls of buffalo and leopards, the trumpeting of elephants or the soft, plaintive cooing of doves and many other unnamed but beautiful sounds. The appearance of the trumpet was unimportant. What mattered was the sound it produced.

The women and children had shut themselves into their huts before the young men arrived with the trumpet. As they entered, each of the unmarried youths had one hand upon the musical instrument (pipe), thus symbolising their unity. All the men then sat together around the kumamolimo fire, singing and eating the food from the basket. No male in the camp was permitted to absent himself from this time of conviviality. Eventually the trumpet was returned to its hiding place in a distant stream and the men returned to their huts. This procedure was repeated nightly for two months. Singing in unison was a primary activity, the apparent purpose being to affirm the laws of the forest, according to which akami was eliminated by the presence of ekimi.

If the molimo festival is an affair for men, the elima is the women's ceremony. It is held after a girl's first menstruation and is an occasion when the whole camp, as well as outsiders, join in the celebration. As soon as a young girl's menses begin, she and all her friends retire to a secluded hut where they are taught the arts and crafts of womanhood and learn to sing the song of the women. It is a time of joy and gladness and other pygmy groups come from all around to pay their respects. Young men loiter about the area, hoping to see young girls who might be eligible future wives. This, of course, is a preliminary step which culminates in marriage and child-bearing.

It is, however, much more than just a rite of passage in that it recognises and attempts to dissolve the potential for conflict inherent in male-female opposition. At the ceremony itself a 'tug-of-war' game, played by adults, symbolises and deals with this opposition. At the beginning of the game, all the men are on one side and all the women on the other, but as one side begins to win, a woman will leave her side to go and help the men if they are losing, or vice versa. Eventually both sides are such a mixture of male and female members that everyone falls to the ground together, laughing and joking, and it is acknowledged that no one wins. The essential unity of all members of the camp, both male and female, is thus jokingly acknowledged, and everyone can get on with the business of living.

At the age of puberty, pygmy males often participate in a village circumcision ritual called *nkumbi*. According to Turnbull (1961:217), although this rite seems to be primarily of Bantu origin, the pygmies willingly submit to it and thereby become 'blood brothers' of those village youths who undergo the ritual at the same time.

Turnbull (1961:147-154) also describes a 'healing ritual' for a young married woman who was childless. An old, old woman was brought in from a neighbouring village, with her husband. They stayed for a few days, during which time nightly vigils were held around the camp fire. There were singing and dancing before the old woman entered into trance, she and the childless young woman dominating the scene.

The holistic approach which characterises the Mbuti way of life in the forest is undoubtedly a primary reason for the fact that they have managed to exist for so long in their isolated circumstances. Nevertheless, as the outside world begins to encroach upon their territory - especially in recent years of warfare in the Ituri forest area - the pygmies are showing an amazing ability to adapt to their changing circumstances. Turnbull (1983:157) suggests that this may be because they have learned to avoid the mistake of bemoaning the loss of the past and to accept the reality of the present. Surely this attitude, together with many others, is worthy of emulation.

SUGGESTED READING

Turnbull, C 1961. *The forest people.* New York: Simon & Schuster.

Turnbull, C 1983. *The Mbuti pygmies: change and adaptation.* New York: Holt, Rinehart & Winston.

Bailey, R C 1989. The Efe: archers of the African rain forest, in *National Geographic* 176 (5).

Dupré, W 1975. *Religion in primitive cultures: a study in ethnophilosophy.* The Hague: Mouton. pp151-190.

CHAPTER 6

The Yoruba of West Africa

In this chapter the multifaceted religious structure of the Yoruba people is reviewed and attention is given to such concepts as: *Olorun, orisha, Ifa* divination, *Egungun* and other ancestral societies, as well as practices associated with the transitional stages of life such as birth, marriage and death.

HISTORICAL REVIEW

In concluding the selective review of various African religions this chapter deals with one of the largest cultural groups on the continent, the Yoruba. Their numbers in 1982 were estimated at between ten and twelve million people, residing in four states of the Nigerian Federation. In the states of Ogun and Oyo they constitute almost the entire population, and in the states of Lagos and Kwara they are the dominant group.

Before European intervention resulted in the creation of the countries Nigeria and Dahomey, the Yoruba were divided among numerous city states, each with its own king or *oba*. Urbanisation thus began at an early stage of their development; nevertheless the majority of the people remained agriculturists. Each city state was protected by walls against outside attack, comparable with the situation obtaining in the land of Canaan when the ancient Hebrews entered the territory. Like the Shona, the Yoruba peoples did not initially conceive of themselves collectively as a people, and there was no single descriptive name for them prior to the nineteenth century. Nevertheless there are many factors, both linguistic and cultural (e g shared traditions), which point to a common origin.

It would seem that the history of the Yoruba people is very ancient indeed. They were famous for their leather work, wood carving, ore smelting, manufacture of steel tools, spinning and other arts long before the intrusion of Western civilisation (Lucas 1948:8). The west coast of Africa is the area from which the reprehensible slave trade drew most of its human 'wares' in the 1700s. Prior to that time slavery was practised by the Yoruba themselves against debtors, criminals and war captives. It would seem, however, that these were generally well-treated.

Slaves imported to America from this area made a strong impact, not only upon that land, but upon the entire world. One of the most famous of them, Booker T Washington, was a brilliant scholar who founded the Tuskagee Institute in the American South. Negro spirituals, which were sung by the slaves of America and subsequently gained popularity worldwide, undoubtedly originated in Yorubaland. Even today, in such places as Cuba, Brazil and New York City, descendants of the Yoruba still practise various forms of their ancient religion.

Numerous attempts have been made to trace the origins of Yoruba culture and religion. In a publication dating back to 1948, Dr J Olumide Lucas expresses his conviction that their roots lie in ancient Egypt. This view is based on what he considers to be etymological similarities between their language and Egyptian hieroglyphics and on seeming parallels in respect of the following cultural and religious concepts: the idea of a future life and judgment after death; the deification of kings; the importance attached to names in determining a person's character; the terms *ba* and *ka* in connection with life after death; belief in ancestral guardian spirits; and the survival of Egyptian-sounding place names and customs, especially in regard to polygamy and burial practices.

More recent scholars have not upheld Lucas's findings and have expressed growing scepticism about the whole tradition of migration (Ferguson 1970:20). Others suggest that the Yoruba may have entered the present area from a northwesterly direction, travelling down the Niger and possibly crossing it in the Borgu area (Beier 1982:4). Although none of these theories has as yet gained precedence over the others, all of them present tantalising possibilities, epitomising the enigmatic character of the Yoruba's origins.

Both archaeological evidence and oral traditions indicate that the major Yoruba kingdoms, which still dominate politically, were probably founded prior to or during the sixteenth century. The Yoruba have a highly complex civilisation which is reflected in their religious beliefs and practices. Theirs is very obviously a religion with a long history of development and change. As is the case with most peoples, religion is the key to an understanding of the Yoruba people.

The real keynote of the life of the Yoruba is their religion. In all things they are religious. Religion forms the foundation and the all-governing principle of life for them (Idowu 1962:5).

Although a great variety of myths and related beliefs are current among the Yoruba, one that is universally subscribed to is the myth proclaiming Ile-Ife (or just Ife) as the original home of the human race. This was where creation supposedly took place and where the first heroic king, Oduduwa, settled. It is the centre of the world, the holy city, the ancestral home of all Yoruba.

According to one version of the myth, Oduduwa had seven sons, to each of whom he gave a beaded crown before he died. They became the original rulers of the seven kingdoms: Ijebu, Ondo, Ilesha, Ketu, Save, Benin and Oyo. Although not all Yoruba agree on how many or which kingdoms were established by the original sons of Oduduwa, everyone believes that only a direct descendant of Oduduwa can be called by the title *oba* and be privileged to wear the sacred beaded crown. Oduduwa's descendants have proliferated, so that today there are 700 or more who bear this title and the concomitant rights and privileges - particularly that of wearing an elaborately beaded crown.

CULTURAL REVIEW

In addition to the holy city of Ile-Ife, other important urban centres of Yorubaland are Oyo, which became an important military base in about the fifteenth century, and Ibadan, which claimed to be the largest city in tropical Africa in 1970 with a population of about a million (Ferguson 1970:21).

Yorubaland has, in general, a humid tropical climate, which is nevertheless cooler than adjacent areas. Peasant farming predominates, with a variety of crops - mainly cassava, maize and yams - raised on relatively small plots. Other crops include kola nuts, okra, beans, cocoyams, peppers, groundnuts, pumpkins, melons, gourds and so on. Bananas, plantains and citrus fruits also flourish. Planting and harvesting of major crops often coincide with religious festivals, which are believed to ensure a continuing abundance of food.

There is no such thing as individual land ownership among the Yoruba. In theory all the land belongs to the king, who apportions it to the various lineages for division among their members. Individual Yoruba thus have the right to use land and reap what it produces, but the land itself cannot be purchased or sold, any more than the air or the sky above.

Traditionally Yoruba society was polygamous, although Christianity now claims many adherents who practise monogamy. People generally live in individual dwellings, clustered together in a square or circle behind a wall. In the centre is an open area which is used by everyone in the compound. More than one family may share a compound, although usually the families are related, however distantly.

In a traditional household each wife has her own home which she shares with her children. The senior wife has authority over the other wives, although the man is the patriarch. A family unit consists of a wife and her children rather than a man, his wives and his children. Lineage is of extreme importance among the Yoruba, regulating the acquisition of land, suitable marriage partners and many other things. Lineages include both ancestors and living relatives. As with the Zulu and other Bantu peoples of southern Africa, the lineage head, who is the senior living member of the group, exercises considerable authority in such matters as discipline, economic support and leadership at religious ceremonies (Ferguson 1970:25).

As might be expected of numerous people who trace their origins to different independent city states, there are many variations in customs, dress and language. Nevertheless the Yoruba people are united by many beliefs and practices. Beier (1982:14) speaks of an evident 'unity in diversity' which is fundamental to an understanding of the people as a whole.

Ferguson (1970:26) singles out three traits for special mention. The first is the extreme hospitality and social politeness observable in, among many other customs, the manner of greeting. These greetings may take several minutes and are specialised, depending on what the persons in question are doing. Secondly, the Yoruba have a high regard for cleanliness. The men are clean-shaven and the women plait their hair in tiny pieces to form ornamental patterns. They are almost always attractively attired, the men wearing robes when they are not dressed in Western-style clothing. Thirdly, the Yoruba often display a certain reticence in their approach to situations or problems. They are not normally boisterous in their behaviour, but are cautious, often using ambiguous language to disguise their true feelings.

The goal of Yoruba life is to achieve holistic unity in the midst of the multiplicity of forces that shape people's circumstances. Beier (1982:14) observes this in the political sphere, where unity is forged by allegiance to the mythological concepts surrounding Ile-Ife and Yoruba kingship, as well as the unifying function of the *oba* within each city state. Socially the Yoruba are unified by their lineage associations, as well as by membership of *orisha* cult groups, despite the multiplicity of orisha that can be worshipped and the resultant diversity of cultic groups.

It is a person's lot to accept the myriad forces that influence human lives and destinies. In themselves these forces are neither good nor bad. They simply exist. One should not try to overcome them but should simply accommodate oneself to them.

Thus unity and spiritual harmony or composure (referred to as *tutu* or 'coolness') are the main goals of life. They can be attained to a considerable degree by observing certain rituals and by consulting a cultic priest - especially the *babalawo* of the Ifa cult - when life seems unbalanced. Priests are specialists trained to deal with ancestral and other spirit beings who might be responsible for discord.

It would be entirely incorrect, however, to describe the Yoruba approach to life as passive or static. Their concept of the Supreme Being, for example, seems to be that of a pulsating life force, present in all people and permeating the entire universe. It is recognised in family and lineage relationships, which disregard human mortality to include the ancestors. This vital force is evident in the Yoruba's ways of self-expression. They demonstrate powerful creativity in such art forms as carving (especially masks), intricate bead designs and dancing (Ferguson 1970:35).

Present-day Yoruba are strongly influenced by both Islam and Christianity. According to a census taken in 1952, four-fifths of the population had, at that time, embraced one or other of these two major world religions (Eades 1980:118). This, however, is not the whole story. Yoruba traditional religion still underlies many of the belief systems prevalent among the people. These underlying tenets have been strong enough to change, in many respects, the character of Islam and Christianity as practised in Yorubaland. One phenomenon in which the strength of traditional religion is particularly evident is the number of people who continue to consult the *babalawo* of the Ifa cult when they are in need of help or advice.

It is, however, with the traditional religious orientation of the Yoruba that this chapter is concerned.

THE RELIGIOUS ORIENTATION OF THE YORUBA PEOPLE

Yoruba religion has been rather extensively researched. At least two problems present themselves when an attempt is made to consolidate the material. In the first place, much of the research is localised and refers to one particular area or group of Yoruba-speaking people. The various accounts do not always agree, since, as has been pointed out, there is considerable diversity among the various Yoruba groups. Parrinder, however, as early as 1949, gave a consolidated review of the major religious characteristics of the entire area in *West African religion: a study of the beliefs and practices of Akan, Ewe, Yoruba, Ibo, and kindred peoples*.

In the second place, Western scholars, in an attempt to come to grips with Yoruba religion, have tended to categorise their findings to such an extent that the religion often appears to be highly systematic and coherent. This is probably not an entirely correct presentation of the facts. As with every religion, especially those which are traditionally oral rather than written, there is a strong element of individual understanding and interpretation.

Nevertheless, we shall attempt, with due recognition of these impediments, to review the religion. To this end it is necessary to categorise and attempt to systematise, as other authors have done. This review of Yoruba religious orientation is presented as more or less representative of West African religion.

Olorun/Olodumare

Most writers on Yoruba religion indicate that the Yoruba believe in a supreme deity identified as *Olorun* or *Olodumare*, who is understood to be the origin and ground of all that exists. The principal divinities were all created by him to be his ministers, so that they might carry out the various functions connected with the creation of the earth and its maintenance (Idowu 1962:18).

The attributes of omnipresence, omniscience and omnipotence are ascribed to this supreme being. He is believed to be a just and impartial judge, as well as the ultimate owner of the human spirit. Known as the lord of the sky or heavens, he is far more than merely a deification of the earth or just another nature god. The name *Olodumare* indicates 'the exalted one to whom I must go or return' (Lucas 1948:41).

The name Olodumare has always carried with it the idea of One with whom man may enter into covenant or communion in any place and at any time, one who is supreme, superlatively great, incomparable and unsurpassable in majesty, excellent in attributes, stable, unchanging, constant, reliable (Idowu 1962:36).

The popular name for this supreme deity, *Olorun*, is composed of two parts: *ol*, meaning chief, ruler or owner; and *orun*, the heavens. He is sometimes referred to in liturgy and in the Odu corpus (a body of divination recitations) as *Olofin-orun*, which conveys a similar idea of a supreme sovereign in heaven. It does not imply that he was conceived of as a personification of the sky, but rather that the sky was understood as being the gateway to the heavens, the abode of Olodumare/Olorun.

Not only is Olorun believed to have created all the other divinities; he was also responsible for the creation of the earth and its original inhabitants. There are numerous variations of this creation myth, but all of them indicate that, although Olodumare did not himself do the work, he provided the impetus for the creation of the earth and its inhabitants. He sent *Obatala* to accomplish this task. One version tells that he gave Obatala (or *Orisha-nla*) the necessary material and tools for the work of creation: some loose earth, a five-toed hen and a pigeon. Obatala immediately set the hen and pigeon to work scattering loose earth over the desolate waste of precreation. He then reported on the progress to Olodumare, who sent the chameleon to inspect the work. After a second visit, the chameleon reported that the work of creation could begin at Ile-Ife. This work was completed in four days; the fifth day was set aside for worship and rest. Later it was discovered that the supply of water was insufficient for creation and, upon Obatala's appeal for help, Olodumare caused rain to fall upon the earth. Only Olodumare could give the breath of life to the human forms which Obatala had fashioned from the dust of the earth (Idowu 1962:19,20).

Olodumare/Olorun can be considered a withdrawn god (*deus otiosus*) in one respect: no temple or cults are dedicated to his worship. His position is very much like that of the traditional kings or obas who work through their ministers. Traditionally, however, in some parts of Yorubaland, a worshipper could occasionally be seen marking out a circle with ashes or white chalk (symbolising eternity) on the ground. Having made a libation of water, the person would place a kola-nut on a piece of cottonwool at the centre of the circle. He would then pick up the kola-nut and, having broken it in the prescribed manner, would hold both halves of the nut aloft in the hollow of his hands as if offering them to the sky, before throwing them down in the centre of the circle once more (Ferguson 1970:37).

Although this custom has died out in most places, it is still incorrect to describe Olorun as a withdrawn god, since he is known and accorded ultimate respect throughout Yorubaland. It can, in fact, be asserted that the belief in the existence of Olodumare/Olorun is the foundation of the whole of Yoruba religion (Idowu 1962:18).

The orisha

Orisha (*orisa*) is a Yoruba word which can best be translated as deity, divinity, god or goddess. Although the Yoruba are said to have 401 such divinities, this is probably not intended as an exact figure, but merely as a way of expressing a number which cannot be counted exactly, much like the English expression 'a thousand and one'.

Many of these deities occupy a more prominent place and have more devotees in one city or geographical area than in another. Thus the list of orisha which one might compile would differ, for example, from Ibadan to the Ondo area. Some orisha are worshipped by a single lineage group in a single town, while others are known and worshipped, to a greater or lesser degree, throughout Yorubaland. Some are personifications of natural phenomena or of attributes of Olodumare, while others are divinised heroes who have been accorded cosmic status and could thus be considered an extension of the Yoruba belief in ancestors.

Each Yoruba town has one or more shrines dedicated to a particular orisha, with attendant priests wearing distinctive robes and insignia. These shrines may take the form of an elaborate temple; more commonly they are simply groves on the outskirts of town or a simple shrine near the home of the priest. Devotees of a particular orisha have to observe special food taboos and make prescribed sacrifices. Each orisha cult has its own rituals, music, oral literature, dances and divination techniques.

Traditionally veneration of a certain orisha was seemingly connected with a person's lineage. However, people only became members of the cult of that orisha if they were called through dreams and a sickness which included spirit possession.

Each orisha is worshipped in three major ways. Daily private rituals are observed in the home, usually early in the morning. Secondly, rituals are conducted every four or eight days (according to the Yoruba four-day working week) at the shrine of the orisha, usually out of doors. Finally annual festivals are held in honour of each orisha. These are elaborate community affairs which also attract devotees from elsewhere.

The list of orisha discussed below is by no means complete. The presentation is merely intended to give an overview of divinities which are worshipped extensively throughout Yorubaland and which are therefore representative of the tenor of Yoruba religion in general.

Obatala (or *Orisha-nla*) and *Oduduwa*

We have already noted that this god was commissioned by Olodumare to perform the work of creation. Tradition holds that he is the vice-regent of Olodumare; as such, he takes precedence over all other deities. He is a popular god, especially favoured by peasants and often described in anthropomorphic terms. A variety of myths surround him, many of them creation stories. One variation indicates that he became drunk on palm wine and was relieved of the duties of creation when Olodumare realised that he had created some people imperfectly.

He is held responsible for the formation of children in the womb and thus all physical defects are his doing. Albinos especially are dedicated to his worship. He is considered to be the protector of town gates and symbolises ritual purity and ultimate good. His worshippers wear white clothing, eat white food, abstain from eating red meat, and offer the white kola-nut in sacrifice.

Sometimes the female aspect of the orisha *Oduduwa* is connected with Obatala. This deity has a somewhat androgynous character, being worshipped as a male deity by some and as a female by others. As the chief female deity she is held to be the wife of Obatala. Their union symbolises the union of earth and sky, which is represented by two whitened calabashes so closely fitted together as to appear inseparable. Thus they are seen as the joint progenitors of the human race.

As a male deity Oduduwa was connected with traditions surrounding the obas or political heads of the city states. In this aspect he is understood to be the son of Olodumare and ancestor of the Yoruba people, first ruler of Ife and progenitor of the human race. This male aspect of Oduduwa predominates throughout Yorubaland today, although the weaker female tradition persists.

Orunmila (or Ifa)

As the alternative name of this god indicates, the most popular cult in all of Yorubaland is founded on him. He is the chief counsellor of the gods who has symbolically taken over the wisdom of Olodumare so that he can play a crucial part in the affairs of the world. Myths portray him as the embodiment of law, order and harmony. Because he knows that the ultimate end of the world is destined to be good, he works to preserve it against attacks by evil forces.

The Ifa system of divination is the channel for communication between human beings and divinities, offering them reassurance in a world that is both bewildering and terrifying. Orunmila/Ifa therefore represents the security that results from balance and wholeness. The Ifa oracle and divination system will be discussed in more detail below.

Eshu

This orisha, a baffling figure, can be seen as the counterpart of Orunmila. Whereas Orunmila is symbolic of order and consistency, Eshu represents the power of mischief and all that is unpredictable. Consequently he is regarded with fear and dread. He is an ambiguous character, being both a rewarder and a punisher of human deeds. He is represented in a variety of ways: by a stone slab stuck into the ground at an angle, by an earthenware pot with a hole in the middle of the base, by a pillar of mud, or by household images made of mud which depict him anthropomorphically, naked, sitting on his feet with bent knees and folded arms. Offerings that may be given to him include cowry shells, cocks and male goats. The blood of a sacrificial animal (in former times possibly of human beings) is sprinkled upon the shrine or image of Eshu and he is understood to be responsible for carrying sacrifices to the other divinities.

Although he has been called a 'trickster' god, no doubt the philosophical concept underlying his character is that, since both good and evil come from Olodumare, one of his ministers must represent those unexpected forces that disrupt human affairs. Misfortune and destruction are his work, but the resulting friction stimulates progress, so that Eshu is not wholly malicious. He is depicted as a wild, lone figure who is continually speeding across the world in pursuit of his official, nefarious business.

Shango

This is the god of thunderstorms who, although feared, is very popular throughout Yorubaland. Tradition holds that Shango was the fourth king of the Yoruba people at Oyo. He was driven to hang himself but rose again and ascended to the sky. Very likely this tradition is historically related to the king, Alaafin, who committed suicide. There may well have been a severe thunderstorm immediately after his death. In any case, Shango is called 'the rage of Olorun' and is conceived of as a destroyer who hurls his thunderbolts and sends down fire at will.

In some parts of Yorubaland, when a house has been hit by lightning, the priests of Shango are summoned. The occupants of the house must not sleep on the premises until the priests have found and removed the 'bolt', which is understood to be a neolithic celt (an axe-shaped stone).

The little gourd, Sere, is sacred to the worship of Shango. According to a myth, the gourd went to certain of the orisha, seeking someone whom she could serve. She was sent to Shango who was so fascinated by the sound she made that he commanded that respect be paid to her. She has been used in rites in his worship ever since (McClelland 1982:23).

Shango is also connected with healing and there is often a pot of water in his temples for sick people to drink or wash themselves. This is called 'the water of life' and the god is understood to be its owner.

Ogun, Oko and Sopona

Although these orisha are not universally worshipped throughout Yorubaland, they are of major importance in certain areas. Ogun is acclaimed as the god of war and iron in numerous places, and in Ondo he is known as the god of thunder. He is the patron of hunters, soldiers and blacksmiths. It is believed that human sacrifices were offered to him formerly in times of severe national crisis. The dog is sacred to him and is used in sacrifices in his honour, along with sheep, goats and fowls. Any piece of iron, from a pin to a limousine, may be presented to him. Many private homes in Ondo have small shrines made of scrap iron and dedicated to Ogun.

Oko, a phallic orisha, is the god of the farm, agriculture and the harvest. Honey bees, symbols of happiness, are his messengers. He is worshipped particularly by women, and his priestesses, who outnumber priests, belong to a type of secret society. Oko is understood to be an arbitrator of disputes, especially those arising among women. An annual harvest festival is held in his honour, at which time immorality abounds. The new moon is also connected with his worship.

Sopono, the god of the disease smallpox, is one of the orisha who inspired great terror and dread in former times. His worship was forbidden during the period of British rule in Nigeria because of the apparent connection between the actions of his priests and the spread of the disease. He is believed to have sprung from the body of Yemoja (a female deity, queen of witches and connected with fish and rivers). His worship was formerly conducted in temples and shrines located in bush areas outside the towns and villages, where it was believed that he held sway since the open spaces of the earth are under his jurisdiction. When a person died from smallpox, the relatives were forbidden to mourn but had to cheerfully accept what was held to be the work of Sopono.

Ancestral spirits and secret societies

As indicated, the divinities discussed above represent only a few of the major, more popular orisha. There are myriad others, including nature spirits, witches and spirit counterparts of humans (e g the *abiku* spirits of born-to-die children). One very important and powerful group of spirit beings is the ancestral spirits.

Since this chapter is written from a Western cultural perspective, an attempt is made to categorise these various spirit beings. In all likelihood the Yoruba themselves do not do this. The spirit realm, which is invisible, nevertheless exerts a strong influence, as real as world crisis situations which a Western person watches or hears about in news bulletins. A Yoruba accepts that at death a person enters the spirit realm as one of the living-dead. Eventually such a spirit may even become a divinity, although not all do; nor are all divinities necessarily former ancestors - the dividing line between them is vague. Those who have departed this world have simply exchanged this life for another. They have unlimited potentialities which can be used to the benefit or detriment of their people remaining on earth. It is, therefore, wiser to keep the ancestors in a state of contentment. Such an attitude to the departed does not necessarily constitute worship, but is rather a manifestation of an unbroken family relationship between a parent who has departed this world and the offspring who are still here (Idowu 1962:192).

The Yoruba have organised secret societies as the primary means of remembering the ancestral spirits. As a rule membership of these societies is restricted to males. In fact, it was formerly claimed that women and others who are uninitiated into the cults could be executed for infractions, which amounted to unwelcome intrusion into cultic activities. This, of course, is not the case with the orisha cults, where women are often in the majority.

As with the orisha, only a few of the major, more popular ancestor societies are reviewed here.

The Egungun society

The name *Egungun*, meaning 'skeleton', at once indicates that this is a cult in remembrance of those who have died. Emotions of affection and reverence seem to characterise the attitude towards the spirits expressed through the cultic medium, in contrast to the dread and fear evident in some of the other cults.

The Egungun society is dedicated to numerous ancestral spirits who may appear at any time, but especially on important occasions. Although the cult occurs throughout Yorubaland, it is particularly popular in Ibadan, where an annual Egungun festival is held at the beginning of the yam harvest early in June. Prior to this occasion, when sacrificial gifts of yams, maize, firm porridge and bean cakes are brought, the harvesting of yams is forbidden. During the weeklong festival, masked men representing Egungun spirits appear in public. Coloured cloth or sackcloth completely covers their bodies, and their faces are hidden by either a wooden mask or a transparent cloth, in such a way that they can see but not be seen.

These masqueraders are considered to be visitors from heaven and may appear frequently at times other than the festival. They assume the identity of dead people and speak in falsetto or guttural voices. They may represent specific ancestors (especially during the burial ceremony held forty days after the death of a loved one) or simply the broad category of ancestral spirits in general. Only authorised persons may come close to or touch one of these spirit figures, but they enjoy great popularity, due, no doubt, to the anonymity which allows great scope for acting and mimicry (Parrinder 1953:46).

Egungun shrines or groves are common in Ibadan and consist of a large shrub, at the foot of which a broken pot may be found. An iron rod is said to be buried beneath this pot and masqueraders assemble at these holy places.

The Gelede guild

The masked figures of this ancestral society appear only on festive occasions. Unlike the Egunguns, Gelede figures are not connected with specific funeral rituals. Although the dancers are masked, their identity is no secret. Their dress is generally smarter and more artistic than those of Egunguns, and the masks are intricately carved to represent people, animals, birds or reptiles. Their dances are popular and highly entertaining. Often the Gelede figures assume female shapes with large breasts, plaited hair, ear-bangles, et cetera. Although often grotesque, their appearance causes general amusement rather than fear.

The Oro cult

Unlike the other two cults described above, the Oro cult arouses great fear among the Yoruba. The spirit-god Oro, said to be the brother of Shango, is the mythological head of the cult. He makes his voice heard by means of a bull-roarer (a flat piece of wood, twirled around at the end of a cord), which is sometimes heard even in the city of Ibadan. This secret society belongs to the bush and its activities are generally nocturnal. It is a strictly male society and whenever the Oro are on the prowl women must stay indoors. This applies especially during the weeklong festival for the dead held in certain areas.

Adherents of this cult claim to be the sole possessors of the knowledge of the Oro mysteries. They alone have the right to perform the Oro ceremonies, which are jealously guarded from the view of the uninitiated. Formerly this cult was responsible for the execution of criminals and other antisocial people who had been condemned by the council of elders.

The Ifa divination system

Perhaps the most widespread cult of all is that of the Ifa divination system. Strictly speaking it is neither a secret society, nor is it devoted to the remembrance of the ancestors.

Ifa is commonly referred to as a cult or an oracle, but just as it is not strictly speaking a cult, it is also not an oracle in the same sense as, for example, the ancient Greek oracle which was located at Delphi. It could, perhaps, be more accurately compared to the I Ching system of divination. Ifa divination is understood to have originated in Ile-Ife, the centre of the Yoruba world, and is associated with Orunmila (or Ifa). Its divinatory practices, however, have spread throughout Yorubaland and even beyond its borders to such countries as Brazil and America. People who are apprehensive about some perplexing situation seek advice from a male priest of the Ifa cult, called a babalawo.

The babalawo or seer is initially called to his divinatory work through an illness or dreams, indicating that certain spirits desire to 'possess' and use him as their 'host'. Subsequently he undergoes a lengthy period of discipline and training, during which he memorises the many *odus* of the Ifa corpus.

The Ifa system of divination is extremely complicated and is based on sixteen basic and 256 derivative figures, called odus. The divination is accomplished by either the manipulation of sixteen palm nuts or the toss of a chain made from seed shells. When palm nuts are used, a whitened circular or rectangular board or fan is placed on a mat. The babalawo diviner, bare to the waist, sits next to the board. He takes the sixteen palm nuts in both hands, places them against his chest and utters an incantation. The nuts are then held in one hand and passed rapidly to the other. If one nut remains, two vertical marks are traced in the white powder on the board; if two nuts remain, a single mark is made. If no nuts or more than two remain, the nuts are rapidly transferred from hand to hand again. This continues until there are eight single or double strokes arranged in two columns. This double eightfold sign represents a legend or verse (an oracle) which the babalawo has learned, following a long line of tradition. This oracle is then adapted to fit the immediate situation of the client.

The divination figure which is formed is called an odu which means chief, head or deity. Each of the sixteen principal odus has sixteen subordinate odus, permitting a possible combination of 256. These 256 have further subordinate odus, bringing the total number of possibilities to 4 096, for each of which there is an appropriate story or couplet.

Although the Ifa divination system is by far the most popular in Yorubaland, there are other deities which are also consulted for oracular answers. The most important of these is the orisha Opele, whose advice is generally less expensive to procure and who is considered to be Ifa's messenger. Divinations may also be obtained by the use of ceremonial water, lustral water (whereby a child is sent into a trance) or by looking at the ground. These three methods are called *wiwo nkan* (looking at something) (Lucas 1948:286).

The consultation of oracular divination devices is one of the ways in which the Yoruba translate their beliefs into their everyday affairs of living. In addition worship through prayer and the giving of sacrifices is also a part of their religious action.

Priests, prayers and places of worship

The initial level of mediation between the human and the spiritual realms is conducted by the heads of families. Each household maintains certain ancestral and protective divinity shrines. It is the duty of the head of the family to represent his household before these shrines daily. As families grow, they divide and this gives rise to the compound, composed of several families with one common shrine dedicated to a unifying ancestor. The eldest male in the family represents the entire group before the shrine in daily prayers. This type of hierarchical religious representation is extended beyond the immediate lineage level to include related compounds and wards.

In addition to these priestly activities performed by lineage heads, numerous individuals are 'called' to become devotees of the various orisha. These may be considered as belonging to at least four categories, although the distinctions between the groups are not always clear-cut. Priests (*olorisha* or those possessed by orisha) are usually attached to temples or are in charge of shrines and are permitted to offer sacrifices to the orisha. In addition, various devotees, who, more often than not, are women, are likewise attached to temples. They are referred to as *iya-orisha* or wives of the orisha and generally act as mediums in the transmission of messages from the orisha to humans. As indicated above, babalawo are the diviners who receive messages according to a particular system. Medicine persons (*onishegun*) may be either men or women. Most priests are also diviners and healers but the reverse is not necessarily true (Parrinder 1969:75).

The correct performance of an act of worship is of utmost importance. Priests who have been specially selected for official cultic duties are given extensive training prior to assuming their mediatory role. Usually two or three candidates at a time are apprenticed to a senior priest. Priests are highly respected and have been a major force in maintaining the traditional nature of Yoruba religion. In addition, they have often been responsible for the enforcement of moral conduct. Because many live an out-of-doors existence, near their shrines, it is generally understood that they are better acquainted with medicines for healing, both of a physical and of a spiritual nature.

It has been said, however, that all Yoruba feel themselves to be in the presence of the divinity wherever they are. Such an awareness presumably brings a sense of either security or fear, depending upon the person's concept of the divinity. Worship is highly liturgical and ritualised and only rituals which are performed correctly are believed to be efficacious. An ethical aspect of worship is reflected in the fact that both the priest and the worshipper must be ritually clean. This requires not only physical lustrations, but also purity of heart.

The family head begins each day at the family shrine before he addresses any living member of the household. There he says 'good morning' to the orisha by offering a libation of water and opening a kola-nut to ascertain the direction that the day's activities will take. In addition each fifth, seventh, ninth and seventeenth day is sacred to various orisha. On these days further acts of worship are performed. The most joyous, extended periods of worship, however, are the festivals held annually in honour of the orisha. The head of each community decides the date when such a festival will be held.

Prayers, usually petitions for physical or material blessings, may be offered, not only during official, prescribed times of worship but also by ordinary devotees at any time of day. Postures for prayer include kneeling, standing and facing a shrine, prostration or even the rhythmic movements of the body in dance. Some priests bare their heads and torsos during ritual prayer, wearing only a loin cloth (Idowu 1962:107ff).

Sacrifices or offerings are also a vital part of worship among the Yoruba. On some occasions the sacrificer shares the offering of food with the orisha and even with other humans in a communal meal. Other sacrifices are intended for the deity alone. These are then burnt, exposed to the elements or buried according to a prescribed ritual. In addition to animal sacrifices, human sacrifice was probably considered to have ultimate value in former times. Now, of course, it has been outlawed. Gifts to the gods may consist of meal and drink offerings, money, ornaments, animals, fowls or vegetables.

Although a Yoruba may worship the orisha in any place, sacred sites abound throughout Yorubaland. A shrine is said to represent the face of the divinity. Private shrines may consist of a particular spot in the home which is designated as sacred by a rectangular block, painted or decorated with either red or red and white trimmings.

In addition, of course, there are sacred forests, sacred trees, shrines at the foot of trees, water shrines on the banks of lakes, rivers and streams, and shrines for travellers at crossroads and beside the road or footpath.

Magnificent temples are not constructed for purposes of communal worship, but simple buildings roughly constructed from cement blocks serve as idol-houses in groves near villages or in cities and towns. Uninitiated persons are warned away from these sacred places by means of a red flag or a palm frond positioned nearby. In the case of major, more popular orisha, an additional enclosure may be constructed as a sort of courtyard attached to the simple shrine. Devotees may gather in the courtyard, but only the official priests are permitted to enter the sacred shrine itself.

Birth, marriage and death

Yoruba beliefs are translated into concrete action not only by prayer and worship, but also by ritualised performances associated with the transitional stages of life.

As soon as conception occurs, an unborn child is surrounded by rituals. Among other actions, the Ifa oracle must be consulted to ascertain what foods may be eaten by the mother-to-be and what sacrifices should be made to ensure the safe delivery of the child. Immediately after birth the baby is examined to see what ancestor may be reincarnated in it. Special orisha and concomitant taboos pertaining to each child are indicated by a babalawo. The child's mother must not leave the house for at least a week after giving birth. On the eighth day there is a name-giving ceremony, which includes a sort of baptism when holy water is thrown on the roof of the dwelling in such a way that it falls on the newborn child (Ferguson 1970:28).

Twins are especially revered among the Yoruba. The firstborn is considered to be the younger who was sent out by the elder sibling to inspect the world. All twins have the same names: *Taiwo* for the firstborn and *Kehinde* for the second. The mother rejoices at their birth by dancing through the town where she buys a pair of wooden figures called *ibeji*. These represent the spiritual selves of the twins and offerings are made to them. If one of the twins dies, it is believed to find a home in its image, in which case the figure is fed, washed and clothed as if it were the child itself.

Children who die shortly after birth are called *abiku* or born-to-die children. It is believed that they were simply spirits who entered the world for a brief period before being carried back to their spiritual abode by their fellow spirits. They are regarded with awe and other children born subsequently are given special attention, such as abusive nicknames to indicate to the spirits that they are not worth taking away.

Traditional marriages are not surrounded by elaborate ritual. Since marriages are usually polygamous, the senior wife from the bridegroom's compound and, if possible, another wife call for the intended bride. She is then given a ceremonial blessing by her own family before being taken to her new husband's compound. When she arrives there, the senior wife bathes her legs and then leads her to her husband's room. Until the birth of her first child she is under the tutelage of the senior wife and may visit her parents' compound only after dark during the first three months of marriage.

On the whole Yoruba people calmly accept the fact that all must die. They explain this by referring to *Iku*, created by Olodumare for the specific purpose of recalling individuals when their time on earth is fulfilled. Iku is called 'heaven's bailiff' and death is understood to be the debt which all must pay in return for the gift of life. It is believed, however, that all persons should have the privilege of living a full and complete life. Therefore deep mourning accompanies the death of young persons who have not completed their days on earth.

Traditionally the Yoruba buried their dead in their own huts, although this custom is no longer prevalent. The body was first washed so that no filth would accompany the person into the afterworld. It was then wrapped in a mat and covered with branches or placed on a shelf inside a pit to prevent earth from falling on it. Food, clothing and ornaments might be buried with dead persons so that they would not be hungry or ill-clad in the afterlife. In some areas of Yorubaland small pieces of the deceased's clothing are kept as souvenirs. The body may be paraded through the streets, whereafter mourners attend a feast provided by the dead person's family.

At the burial ceremony, a priest officiates by splitting a kola-nut in a final act of farewell to the dead person. Several days later another ritual is performed which is called 'bringing the spirit of the deceased into the house'. It is performed in the dark of night and a shrine is erected as a continual, communal meeting place between the dead person and the living relatives (Idowu 1962:190,191).

This chapter brings us to the end of our study of five selected traditional African religions. No doubt in the process of reading you have been aware of both differences and similarities between the various orientations. The differences are considerable and point to the fact that it is unwise to attempt an imposition of one unifying framework upon all African religions. It is for this reason that five more or less representative systems were presented in this book for consideration. Nevertheless it is likewise the contention of this book that African traditional religion can be considered as an entity as long as the underlying differences are recognised. Support for this point of view is given in the following chapter.

SUGGESTED READING

McClelland, E M 1982. *The cult of Ifa among the Yoruba*. London: Ethnographica.

Bascom, W 1969. *Ifa divination: communication between gods and men in West Africa*. Bloomington: Indiana University Press.

Idowu, E B 1962. *Olodumare, god in Yoruba belief*. London: Longmans

Parrinder, G 1953. *Religion in an African city*. London: Oxford University Press.

Parrinder, G 1969. *West African religion*. London: Epworth.

CHAPTER 7

THE AFRICAN PATTERN

> Unity and diversity are both characteristic of African religions. In general, however, religion which for African people is coextensive with being human follows a life-affirming, life-sustaining pattern.

Throughout this book an effort has been made to emphasise the twin truths that African people not only had authentic religious practices and beliefs before the arrival of Western civilisation, but that these beliefs were both varied and imbued with profound symbolic value. It must also be borne in mind that because African religions (like all religions) are human institutions, they have been subject to distortion, decay and degeneration over the centuries. During the past 200 years especially, they have been greatly modified by the major world religions with which they have come into contact. Consequently it is not always easy to tell exactly what African people believed before their encounter with the Western world.

In the preceding chapters you were introduced to only five of the multitude of religious systems to be found on the continent of Africa. This chapter gives an overview of African religion in general. Obviously there is no one cultural area or group that can be considered normative for the whole continent. No such norm exists. The religious practices and beliefs throughout this continent developed in independent cultures, often separated from each other by great distances or other geographical barriers. Thus there are, as has been indicated, tremendous differences. The following are merely suggested distinctions which come to the fore and the list is not intended to be comprehensive. A comparative review of other African religious systems would likely produce a somewhat different set of variations.

An initial comparison which immediately presents itself is that between the unsophisticated simplicity of the religious approach of the San and even more particularly of the Mbuti peoples with that of the more complex orientation of the Zulu, the Shona and especially the Yoruba peoples. Even here one cannot simply identify San and Mbuti religious conceptions without further ado. Whereas the Mbuti seemingly have a vague concept of a more or less unidentified creative power at work in the world (possibly more closely related to a principle of life force), the San, in addition to recognition of the power of n/um, have anthropomorphised conceptions of a great and a lesser god whose abodes are metaphorically located in the sky. In addition the San, in contrast to the Mbuti, seem to have definite dualistic tendencies in their religious conceptions.

Likewise the Bantu orientations of the Zulu and Shona cannot simply be equated one with the other, although there are strong similarities between them. One major point of difference seems to lie in the area of spirit possession. Among the Zulu acceptable spirit possession is primarily by ancestral spirits for purposes of healing and divination. Although possession by alien spirits (*amandiki*) occurs, this is generally not welcome and has not been incorporated in an integral way into the belief system. These spirits are not part of tradition, but in fact represent a fairly recent innovation attendant upon the displacement and mobility caused by labour migration. Among the Shona the matter of spirit possession is far more complex. Neither alien spirit possession nor ancestral possession is unwelcome and both have been incorporated into the overall religious structure. Unwelcome possession which does, however, occur (*ngozi* spirits) represents evil and ill-will not dealt with in this life. Other evil beings, the varoyi or witches, likewise metaphorically portray evil, possibly of a jealous nature.

In contrast to the Bantu orientations as represented by the Zulu people, the Yoruba of West Africa show marked differences. Whereas the Zulu (and also to a lesser extent the Shona) conception of the Supreme Being is seemingly more in the nature of a creative force which set the world in action and then withdrew, the West African view is more specifically of an identifiable being who works together with a 'senate' of deities. The attributes of iNkosi which suggest facets of his nature are given by means of praise names. It must be acknowledged, however, that in the light of these praise names iNkosi cannot be viewed entirely as a 'deus otiosus' (or withdrawn god). Olorun's attributes are represented rather by the orisha which work together with him in the maintenance of the world.

Among the Zulu Nomkulbulwana as an earth deity is a unique phenomenon among African religions. Certain present-day scholars of Zulu religion hold the opinion that she represents the truest form of divinity for Zulu people while Mvelinqani/iNkosi are considered to have developed their importance and structure from contact with Western Christian conceptions. The mainstream of scholarly opinion, however, simply views Nomkulbulwana as an additional expression of divinity and Mvelinqani (iNkosi) as a Supreme Creator.

Concerning the secular organisation of religion for purposes of ritual there are likewise marked contrasts between Bantu and West African orientations. Among the Zulu the head of the household performs priestly functions of a familial nature while the headman of a village or the chief of a clan performs these functions for the larger groups. There is no official priesthood as such. The isangoma mediates with the spiritual realm for the necessary maintenance of wholeness and health. Divination is largely by means of ecstatic (trance or dream) communication with the spirits.

Among the Yoruba, in addition to the offering of daily prayers by the head of the family, there is an organised priesthood for purposes of offering sacrifices and tending the cultic temples and shrines. Spirit possession (and thus communication with the invisible realm) is common among devotees of the various orisha. Priests often act as healers and diviners. Divination is more commonly carried out by specific activities as in the Ifa system rather than by relying on ecstatic communication through trance or dream states. However the spirits or divinities are believed to guide the outcome. Belief in the ancestors takes different forms, not only by the way in which they are remembered but also in their status and work after death.

Although these differences are considerable they are to be expected. What is surprising is the amount of similarity which exists regarding underlying religious assumptions across the vastness of the continent. Thus it is not inappropriate to refer to Traditional African Religion as a whole without always emphasising the differences which exist between the various traditions. Both unity and diversity are characteristic of religion - and of all of life - on the African continent. This is borne out by an examination of languages, art, music - in short, by the whole of African culture.

We must remember that African religious traditions were handed down orally from generation to generation. We therefore have no written records to examine. Their 'scriptures' consist of symbolic art or dance forms and practices which have been observed and interpreted, often by outsiders of a different religious persuasion. Religion in African societies has been perpetuated by an almost unconscious process: through the communal religious life of the tribe, the repetition of myths and legends and participation in the cult. For Africans religion is all-embracing: agriculture, social life, the political structure, economics - everything is imbued with religious significance. It follows that there are no irreligious people in a tribal community. To be means to belong. And there is no thought of conversion or change from one tribal religion to another. Having been born into a society, one automatically participates and shares in its religious life.

For African people religion is a necessity and not an option. It provides them with ways of coping with the mysterious realities in their immediate environment - natural forces, ancestral spirits and powers felt to be functioning through the social institutions of the tribe or community. ATR always relates, in an organic and vital way, to the world in which it exists. Its adherents believe that human beings are not the only organisms that matter in the world. African people therefore relate closely to their natural environment and seek to establish harmony with it.

Belief in a transcendent creator is one of the more apparent tenets which African peoples hold in common and which has received considerable scholarly attention. In addition, as has been indicated, the community is the focal point of ATR. Belief in the all-pervasive well-being of individuals in their relationship with their society is therefore customary. What disrupts harmony and wholeness is evil, to be sought out and eradicated. Ancestors and other spirit mediators are the custodians of the community and its continuing well-being. They function to permit this desirable balance to be maintained. Their visible representatives are the traditional diviners and healers who are specially selected for the task of mediation between the spiritual and the physical world. Rites, rituals, sacrifices and prayers are the means by which a harmonious relationship is maintained between the visible and the invisible African community.

More, however, needs to be said about each of these generalised components of ATR.

A SUPREME BEING

Throughout most of Africa there is belief in a Supreme Being who created and set the world in motion and then, more or less, withdrew. Such a God is called a *deus otiosus* or a *deus remotus* and is seldom approached directly by individuals. Communication is normally maintained by spirit mediators, usually the ancestors.

Such an interpretation of the God of Africa immediately raises numerous questions. Should we then consider ATR to be monotheistic? Is the African God in fact a *deus remotus*? Have African concepts of God been influenced by either Muslim or Christian missionaries? Numerous writers and scholars have given a variety of answers to these and other questions, so that it is not always possible to make final statements.

Twesigye (1987:90), for example, asserts that the people of Africa are monotheistic inasmuch as they recognise only one God as the creator *ex nihilo*, the sustainer of everything that has being or existence. In many African religions, however, there appears to be greater emphasis on lesser gods (e g the orisha of the Yoruba) or spirits (ancestral spirits among the Zulu, various spirits among the Shona). When this area of belief is underscored, the tendency is to describe ATR as polytheistic, or, in some instances, pantheist.

None of these terms, however, seems to adequately portray the many nuances which characterise African religion. Since both monotheism and polytheism are words deriving from a Western religiocultural context, it is probably preferable to use neither in referring to African religion. At the very least one can recognise that each of these elements is present in ATR, representing different ways of thinking of the numinous at different levels of experience (Evans-Pritchard 1956:316). It can be correctly stated that ATR incorporates both theism and spiritism in its belief in both a Supreme Being and a general world of spiritual powers.

It has been asserted that there is seemingly no people or tribe in Africa which does not believe in a Supreme Being with one or more names describing him in terms of his activities. While the early missionaries interpreted this Supreme Being more or less as a *deus remotus*, recent African theologians, writing about their own religiocultural background, deny this. They insist that

God is never far from an African's thoughts or perceptions of the world. He is, above all else, the creator of all things, and as such the ground and being of all that is. God is presence, continuing providence, a mysterious power in all things, the one that renders people capable of acting and who consequently holds them morally responsible for their actions (Dupré 1975:69).

In his book, *Concepts of God in Africa* (1970), Mbiti presents an account of widely divergent views held by some 270 African tribes concerning the nature and attributes of God. The result is a systematic categorisation in the Western Christian tradition. Although this attempt has been criticised by some as being oversimplified, it nevertheless supports the theory that the God known to African people prior to the relatively recent advent of Christianity and Islam on the continent was not merely a *deus otiosus*.

Setiloane (1976:77-86) likewise indicates that the idea of a *deus otiosus* was merely Western missionaries' misinterpretation of the traditional African view of the Supreme Being. He considers the African concept of God to be more closely allied to Rudolf Otto's description of God as *mysterium tremendum*. This, he believes, is a more accurate image of the Supreme Being than that presented by Western Christianity.

In many respects the attitude adopted by African people to the Supreme Creator resembles the respect accorded their rulers. Throughout Africa proper procedures must be observed if a person wishes to address a human ruler. An ordinary person cannot simply enter directly into the presence of a chief or king but can do so only indirectly through approved mediators or councillors. This attitude of respect for authority extends to the spiritual arena as well so that intermediaries are necessary if one wishes to address divinity. This is particularly true regarding the Supreme Being who is considered to be behind everything - cattle, animals in general, trees and plant life as well as human beings.

In spite of these attempted generalisations regarding the concept of God in Africa, it is imperative that we remember the variations which occur between the differing traditions, not forgetting that even within a given system there are many individual interpretations. As indicated above there seem to be differing conceptions of the Supreme Being within the five traditions presented in this book. Although the most clearly formulated ideas seem to occur among the Bantu peoples and the West African peoples, these are expressed in different ways. Considerable uncertainty occurs regarding the precise understanding of the nature of the Supreme Being before the arrival of the missionaries among the Bantu groups. On the other hand it is seemingly more firmly established that prior to the arrival of outside influence West African peoples believed in a Supreme Being whose attributes (expressed not only by additional descriptive names but also by means of a pantheon of lesser, serving divinities) appear to be closely allied with those of the Supreme Being in Semitic religions. Among the Mbuti the idea of life force seems to determine thoughts about divinity whereas the !Kung San have, in addition, very definite conceptions about both the great and lesser gods. The mythical creator/trickster of !Kaggen must also be taken into consideration when one is dealing with divinity among the San.

The fact that the Mbuti and the San have been less exposed to Western culture may mean that their concepts are less readily interpretable into Western categories. This does not make their ideas about God any less relevant than another's. It may merely be that the point of identification between the two has not yet been fully explored. Truth about another's belief usually comes to us, not as a revelation of something entirely different, but as something we have known all along and have simply tried to express in another way, so that we say, 'Ah, but that is what I have always believed'. Perhaps such recognition of a common truth shared by the San, the Mbuti and ourselves still awaits us.

SOCIETAL HARMONY AND WELL-BEING

Throughout Africa the milieu in which religious concepts are born and nurtured is that of the tribe or group to which individuals belong. So important is the community to religion that it has itself become a part of the traditional African creed. Whether the individual or the group takes precedence is difficult to determine. Without the group, the individual would not exist, but likewise, the group would be null and void without its individual members. For Africans, however, the community on the whole has primacy, since it is understood to antedate the individual. The community is a priori to existence.

In practice this generally means that a strong emphasis is placed upon kinship. Kinship is reckoned to be a result of both birth and marriage. It controls social relationships between people, governs marital customs and regulations and determines acceptable interpersonal behaviour. It extends to animals, plants and even inanimate objects. In some African groups this relationship is symbolised by totemic regulations, although totemism is not normally as pronounced in Africa as it is among many other primal religions elsewhere in the world.

The community is the arena for human interaction. Tensions arise and must be dealt with, lest they erupt in acts of aggression and surface as sin. It follows that the community is also the arena where forgiveness and reconciliation can and must take place. The crucial requirement, always, is the maintainance of order and balance within the group; no one individual is permitted to disrupt the whole.

Ngubane (1977:28) indicates that for the individual Zulu good health means much more than just a healthy body. It pertains to all that concerns the person including the perception of a harmonious, co-ordinated universe. This could be said about African people throughout the continent. Health, balance, harmony, order, continuity are all key words. They not only describe a desirable present condition for individuals and the community, but also represent the goal towards which people constantly strive. This ideal needs to be maintained not only within the visible community but equally in relation to the invisible community, conceptualised as spiritual powers (e g the ancestors).

This holistic emphasis which is placed upon healing in the ATRs must not be underestimated. Recent findings seem to indicate that pain is a relative concept which differs among people. It can therefore probably be said that within the African context pain is not predominately physical and individualistic, but rather psychical with strong social dimensions. Pain is felt when relationships are disturbed; when problems are encountered in the socioeconomic and political spheres. This truth is borne out by an increase in the number of people who consult diviners and traditional healers as well as those who join Indigenous Churches during times of socioeconomic and political stress.

In the perception of African people Western medicine is often viewed merely as a means of treating symptoms. Unless the cause of an illness is ascertained the treatment is merely superficial. This cause, more often than not, is to be found in an initial and continuing disruption of unity which causes stress both to a given group and to its individual members. Possibly it was this apparent need for holism, which Durkheim recognised in other primal communities, which led him to conclude that society takes precedence, not only historically but also ontologically. This need for a unified view of nature, both one's own inner nature as well as the external nature, including both people and physical surroundings, may be one of the most ancient needs to be recognised by humankind. While it would be most unreasonable to suggest that the modern world revert to primal models of religion, it is not unreasonabale to acknowledge this human need for holistic unity. In recent years the medical profession has been paying increased attention to this factor. Perhaps other groups such as large corporations, financial and educational institutions should do so as well.

Early anthropologists used the term 'animism' in their attempts to come to grips with the spiritual component which seemed to imbue primal people's conceptions of life. Endowed with their own Western traditions they believed that primal people preceived the entire world - inanimate as well as animate - as being alive with spirits or localised forces that could be utilised for either good or evil. On the one hand, this was seen to be an impersonal power residing in all nature; on the other hand, it could become personal since it could be 'tapped' and used. This 'animistic' power could be focused and concentrated in amulets, medicines and words, and enable people to do supernatural things.

Father Placide Tempels (1959:44) probably came much closer to the truth of this concept when he said that the supreme value for Africans is life or force to live strongly. This he called vital force. This concept was referred to as being present among the Mbuti and the Yoruba and probably plays a large role in all African religious outlooks. Without a certain amount of life force a person would die. This vital force is preserved and strengthened by prayers, sacrifices, rituals, wisdom and proper conduct. While there is always the risk that one may lose one's life force, one must take care not to be over-ambitious and attempt to acquire more than one's fair share. Such unbalanced acquisitiveness is manifested by the sorcerer. It is incumbent upon each person to help preserve balance and maintain harmony, even in such matters as the distribution of dynamic life force.

God, the creator, grants to each individual the best possible gift when he gives him life to enjoy. This peaceful enjoyment of life by a person provides a framework and structure for living. That is, an African is born, brought up, trained and guided to maturity so as to be able to achieve and experience fullness of life. At the same time each African is made acutely aware that individual life and happiness are not possible in isolation and apart from other people, because life is something communal and can only be manifested properly and adequately in a network of interdependencies between persons and community. Accordingly, in all life's pursuits, Africans will always strive to maintain a dynamic relationship with the extended family, clan or tribe, including the ancestors, God and nature.

Africans feel obliged to maintain each of these dynamic relationships of existence-in-community. They realise that, because of this communal interdependence, their activities influence and shape their neighbours' lives, whose activities, in turn, influence and shape their own (Maimela 1985:66).

Membership of the community cannot simply be taken for granted. It is perceived as a lengthy process which may begin even before birth. A person's parents may be required to participate in practices and rituals pertaining to courtship and marriage which contribute to the eventual inclusion of their as yet unborn children into the community. Additional rites and rituals may be performed to sustain children's life force during their growing years. Finally, at puberty, they gain full membership of society by undergoing an initiation ritual, which usually involves circumcision for males and sometimes clitoridectomy for females. This life-in-community extends beyond death. Death is seen merely as a further stage of life, in which a person no longer participates physically but becomes a spiritual participant as an ancestor.

Naturally this description of a person's progress through the stages of life is generalised and does not fit all African practice in every detail. Not all African groups, for example, practise clitoridectomy, nor even circumcision, but a sufficient number do to warrant inclusion in a generalised pattern of ritual practices pertaining to an individual's participatory membership of a given community.

Again, ritual practices are more apparent among the Zulu, Shona and Yoruba peoples than among the San or Mbuti. Yet the central truth of the importance of order and harmony, which is the religious principle underlying various ritual practices, is probably even more in evidence among the San and Mbuti than among other African groups.

Societal disruption

That which disrupts the normal flow of life, either of an individual or of the group as a whole, is evil. It must be avoided if possible; if not, the cause must be ascertained and a remedy sought so that vital force can be restored. This process of defending itself continuously against disruption becomes a major factor in binding the community together and keeping it intact.

Among almost all African groups certain persons are specially selected by powers (usually the ancestors) in the invisible spirit world for this mediatory work. These chosen individuals are the diviners and traditional doctors. Among the fears that beset Africans are fear of evil spirits and malicious persons called witches or sorcerers, who use medicines to harm and destroy; fear of offending the ancestors; and fear of losing one's vital force. In addition, of course, anxieties are triggered by natural disasters, drought, lack of fertility and, increasingly, by the complexities encountered by those who have attempted to settle in urban areas.

In Semitic religions this source of evil is conceptualised as the devil or satan. African religions, especially among the Bantu groups, tend to locate the source of disruptive evil in the human world, in the ambitions and jealousies of people. Such people are witches or sorcerers. A person accused of witchcraft (usually a woman) is viewed as being inherently evil. The condition is almost incurable. Witches' activites are often nocturnal and they are seen as antisocial individuals during the daytime. Many African groups believe that witchcraft is inherited, passed down the female line from one generation to the next.

Sorcerers are those who use evil means to gain advantage only at certain times or in certain situations. Men are more often accused of sorcery than of witchcraft. Anyone can, at any time, be suspected of sorcery, but the most powerful members of the community, often the diviners and traditional doctors themselves, are more prone to such accusations.

Inversion and reversal are recurrent symbolic themes within the general context of demonic humanity as embodied by witches and sorcerers. For example, some groups believe that witches fly backwards, walk on their hands or heads, dance naked, feast on corpses, exhibit insatiable and incestuous lust (despite sexual impotence), murder their relatives, et cetera (Ray 1976:50).

When tensions appear in a community, outwardly manifested in barrenness in women, natural disasters, infertility of crops or animals and the like, witchcraft is suspected. This calls for remedial action. Some remedies are preventive in that their purpose is to avert evil before it occurs. Others are curative and are designed to divert or eliminate the evil which has already infected the community or the individual. The remedies are rites and rituals, which include such things as amulets, sacrifice, dancing and other forms of art. Just what, when and how such remedies should be applied can only be ascertained by those who reside in the spirit realm (ancestors usually) and the message must be communicated to their earthly representatives, the diviners and doctors.

Religious authorities

Ancestors and intermediary spirits

Generally speaking, authority among African people is vested in those whose lives have covered a long period. The elders of the community are moving steadily closer to the time when they will exchange their visible, earthly form for an invisible one. Those who have advanced to a spirit state have more authority than fleshly human beings, just as elders generally have more authority than children.

Mbiti (1969:25) characterises those who have departed the visible world as the 'living-dead', a phrase that encapsulates the essence of African belief about those who have been parted from their community by death. Africans believe that all people should be enabled to live a normal life - that is, they should grow up, marry, bear children and eventually depart this life for a spiritual realm, whence they will protect and direct their earthly relatives. In return, they must be remembered by those still living physically.

This belief in ancestors is most clearly to be seen in the preceding reviews of Zulu and Shona religion, although it also features among the Yoruba. It is less apparent among the beliefs of the Mbuti and the San. In addition to belief in the living-dead, the Yoruba, as has been noted, also have an extensive pantheon of deities to whom they can pray as intermediaries. Generally speaking, where a belief in ancestors predominates, fewer divinities are recognised.

Veneration of the ancestors has been described as a central feature of African religion. Over practically the whole of the continent, with the possible exception of certain tribes, what is known as the ancestor cult is one of the most prominent features of traditional religion.

Spirit beings, whether conceived of as divinities or as ancestors, are in reality intermediaries between humans and the Supreme Being. Just as a chief should not be approached directly without due courtesy, so petitions to God should be directed through the proper channels - neither casually nor without proper consideration. Because the ancestors are recently departed, they are still aware of the needs of their offspring. Because they have matured beyond mere earthly existence, they are closer to God and live in a realm of spiritual realities.

The attitude of people towards the ancestors is often ambivalent. The living-dead are both loved and feared, depending on the circumstances. Once a person has died and joined the realm of spirits, they no longer display human behavioural characteristics. The living-dead are generally expected to be protective and beneficent, even if they were not so during their earthly existence.

Ancestor recognition and remembrance is also often associated with a belief in reincarnation, especially in connection with the chieftainship, for purposes of societal stability. Among those who hold such beliefs, chieftainship is understood to be a kind of sacred kingship in which the position of the king or chief is surrounded by a variety of rules and taboos. Furthermore, while ancestors may continue to inhabit the spirit world, they may, at the same time, be 'reborn' in descendants who display characteristics reminiscent of a recently departed forebear.

One category of people who are never allowed into the spirit world are witches. Their eternal punishment is to be excluded from fellowship and to wander about forever.

Human mediators and healers

Generally speaking, these are the traditional doctors and diviners, whose work is complementary. Often one person fulfils both functions (i.e. divining the cause and prescribing the cure). Whenever evil attacks a community or an individual and the disruption of harmony and well-being becomes evident, a cause is sought by having recourse to the spirit realm. Divination establishes the cause, after which an acceptable remedy is prescribed. This remedy may take the form of a ritualised observance such as the offering of a sacrifice, or of medicines which have symbolic as well as therapeutic value. The remedies sometimes seem to move out of the sphere of religion into that of magic.

Nevertheless, the doctors and diviners who stand between the visible and invisible worlds are greatly feared and respected for the power inherent in their office. They are in touch with a world beyond the visible one and practise and prescribe according to the rules of 'white magic', which restores or maintains the community, in contradistinction to 'black magic', practised by witches and sorcerers, which inflicts disruption and imbalance on society as selfish ends are pursued. As might be expected, although the office of traditional doctors and diviners is one of positive, beneficial value, in practice they, too, may be suspected of sorcery because of their tremendous power and insight.

Other authority figures

In addition to the traditional diviners and doctors who may in certain ways be viewed as the moral analysts of the community, there are other authority figures among African peoples whose work likewise contributes to the maintenance of balance and harmony. From time to time prophetic figures arise who do not seem to support the status quo but call the people to a new kind of life. An example is the prophetess Nongqause, who called on the Xhosa people to kill all their cattle so that a millennium of peace might ensue.

Some African tribes have priests. These were encountered in the discussion of Yoruba cultic groups. The distinctive mark of a priest is his authority in the area of ritual and symbolic action. He may be less ecstatic in his approach than the typical diviner, although this is not always true. Among many African groups the lineage head performs necessary priestly functions for the family.

Sacred kingship is also found among some African groups. In the case of all these authority figures, the real purpose of their activity is the maintenance of harmony within the social group.

Rites and rituals

Not only religious authority figures are concerned with the maintenance of a holistic community. Many actions, performed both intentionally and spontaneously, are directed towards this same goal. Dancing and other art forms are examples of this type of harmony-regulating activity. Africans dance to celebrate every imaginable situation - joy, grief, love, hate, to bring prosperity or to avert calamity. In addition, singing and joyful conversation enable African people to minimise tensions within a closed community. Sometimes the dancing and singing are planned and formal, but more often they are simply a spontaneous expression of emotions.

The African pattern is life-affirming and life-sustaining. As the present millennium draws to a close, it is a pattern that warrants closer attention and in-depth analysis. In the next chapter we suggest possible areas for such transcultural study.

SUGGESTED READING

Taylor, J V 1959. *The primal vision.* London: SCM.

Tempels, P 1959. *Bantu philosophy.* Paris: Presence Africaine.

Setiloane, G M 1986. *African theology: an introduction.* Johannesburg: Skotaville.

EPILOGUE

African religions and the future

It must be acknowledged that, even though African religions have persisted for hundreds and even thousands of years, in recent times they appear to have reached a point of near extinction. Increasingly over the past two centuries Western culture, which developed from a Graeco-Roman background combined with Semitic religious orientations, has come to dominate the world scene. A few points, however, need to be made in this regard.

In the first place, things are not always what they seem to be. Although African traditional religion has often seemed to give way to either Christianity or Islam, on closer analysis it remains discernible as a vital force among African peoples, in much the same way that yeast, which cannot be seen, nevertheless permeates dough and changes its nature. The Independent Church movements which proliferate throughout the continent, but especially in southern Africa, testify to the accommodating adaptability of African traditional religions. But in addition to these, traditional Christianity and Islam have both acquired an 'African visage'. They have been changed by their contact with ATR, just as ATR has been changed by its contacts with Christianity and Islam. A mutual sharing of those concepts which are held to be the essence of truth for the different religions has been taking place on the continent of Africa over the past two centuries.

Scholars, authors, politicians, preachers, the person-in-the-street - all are concerned about the future of the world. Alvin Toffler is one author, among many others, who has written about the near future. He describes it as a time of shock, a third great wave of civilisation superseding the earlier agricultural and industrial eras. This new period has, in fact, already started and is carrying the world forward at an ever accelerating pace. People in Western cultures are confronted with new kinds of family life, with macro-manufacturers who have vested interests in more than one nation, with nations that are fragmenting because of regional or isolationist interests. Old political patterns are becoming obsolete. People are faced with the marvel of the computer, with 'electronic cottages' that all but run themselves, with television that offers the viewer a participatory as well as a passive listening-and-looking role. These are exciting possibilities that beckon from the future.

At the same time the horror of nuclear warfare and nuclear global pollution remain frightening threats to that future. Ecological realities confront humankind even while energy demands are rapidly increasing. New sources of energy are needed, but people dare not denude or pollute the world any further. Discoveries in the field of biogenetics bring both hope and fear. Unknown diseases threaten the future of humankind, at the same time as overpopulation of the globe poses perplexing problems. The pollution which humans have inflicted upon the earth seems to be extending into the atmosphere and perhaps eventually into the universe beyond. The list is endless.

Surely these possibilities and problems are remote from the world of traditional cultures which survive only in isolated corners of the world's continents. But are they? More than ever before, human beings may have arrived at a time in history when the clearest imperative is to know themselves. If that is true, then the greatest challenge facing people today is that of discovering their inner selves. Before humans are overwhelmed by the forces of the future, each person needs to pause, to look within, to attempt to discover what lies at the deepest levels of consciousness - or even below that, in the realm of the subconscious, perhaps even as Jung suggests in the collective unconscious.

It is precisely at this point that a study of African traditional religions may make a significant contribution to the future. There are multitudinous ways in which this may be done. The following suggestions are merely offered as a starting-point. A great deal more can and should be said about each of them but such an undertaking lies beyond the scope of this book.

COMMUNITY SOLIDARITY

The solidarity of the community is a pronounced feature, not only of ATR, but of all primal cultures. If myth can be viewed as a mirror of a people's self-awareness, then the Zulu myth which indicates that people emerged communally from a bed of reeds gives a fair indication of the Zulu people's perception of themselves (Setiloane 1986:9). This is also observable in the way individuals are nurtured. A newborn child becomes a person in and through the community. He or she is far more than just a lone individual, struggling against the forces of nature, but is part of a group, a whole that is more than the mere sum of its constituent parts. In Africa, particularly, every member of society is closely linked with the community. This creates a chain which binds each person horizontally to the other members of the tribe, and vertically to both the deceased ancestors and coming generations. Individuals cannot exist alone. They *are* because they *belong*.

Loneliness may well be one of the most devastating diseases of modern people. The Western emphasis upon individual rights has swung the pendulum so far off-centre that many people are no longer able to recognise their right to belong. Rights imply responsibility, and responsibility means sacrifice - sometimes of one's individual rights. All of this, and more, may be brought home to modern people if they attempt a reconciliation with their fellow human beings in primal societies. A concept of belonging to a community, to a tribe, to a family group, may go a long way towards combating the disease of loneliness which threatens to destroy many Westerners.

Not only are African people traditionally aware of their interrelatedness; they are equally keenly aware of their relationship to all of nature. As Toffler (1983:121) puts it, they are 'stitched into the natural world so closely as to share in the actual "livingness" of animals, trees, rocks, and rivers'. Kushner (1981:67) reminds us that there is a high mathematical probability that some of the molecular stuff that has gone into, is in or will go into what we conventionally call us, has come from or will yet go to the furthest reaches of the cosmos. Furthermore, it is highly probable that some of our molecular stuff has come from the primeval fireball of creation itself, the furnace in which the universe began. He continues to posit that all creation is one person, one being whose cells are interconnected within a medium called consciousness. Mind, therefore, is not simply located in the human skull: animal, vegetable and mineral forms are all alive.

African people have long been aware of this interrelatedness of all that exists.

RITUALS

Rituals in African societies are further proof of their community orientation. A ritual usually demands participation by various tribal members, apart from the individual on whose behalf it is performed. The ritual of initiation particularly provides a helpful means of transition from one status in the community to another. Children are expected to behave in certain ways but, once they have undergone initiation ceremonies, they are fully aware of their new adult status and of the behaviour appropriate to this new role. Similarly marriage rituals provide a means of relinquishing old behavioural patterns and adjusting to new ones.

Rituals often take the form of dramatic presentations among African people. By means of objectifying their inner fears and perplexities the people are enabled to deal with them in a more meaningful and constructive way. In relatively recent times this approach has been utilised in Western cultures as well by psychiatrists working with people in therapy groups.

Likewise psychology has recognised the need for ritual in the lives of all people. Indeed, the need is so pressing that people are constantly inventing new ways to 'ritualise' their lives. A routine greeting to passers-by on the way to work, a daily cup of tea at home or at the office, the celebration of holidays in certain customary ways, wedding ceremonies, funerals - in these and many others ways modern people express their need to add a ritual dimension to their lives. Perhaps if people became more consciously aware of their need for ritual they could fill them with more meaningful content.

Rituals help to structure and thus give meaning to human life. Individuals need this structure lest their lives become totally aimless. When structure breaks down, psychological disaster looms.

SYMBOLISM

Rituals in African cultures are meaningful not only because of their stated, overt purpose - to purify or to facilitate a change in status - but also because they are rich in symbols. They express a community's beliefs, not so much in words as in acts and art forms. In addition myths in ATRs are rich in symbolism and metaphor. According to Soyinka (1976:3), who gives his readers a wealth of information regarding the metaphorical value of certain Yoruba deities, myths arise from people's attempts to externalise and communicate their inner intuitions.

Western people have become increasingly obsessed with a multiplicity of words - printed pages abound more and more; speeches are disseminated world-wide via the television screen. Instead of being powerful vehicles to carry meaning from one person to another, words have lost their meaning more often than not and fall, at last, on deaf ears.

If there is a disease which rivals loneliness in the modern world, it is the lack of valid communication. Words alone, robbed of their import because of their multiplicity, become meaningless symbols. It may be time to look for new symbols, for 'multimetaphors' that will enable people to interpret and give meaning to their lives. A single symbol can say so many things so profoundly to a group, but it can also say them independently to individuals.

In African communities the taboos on certain words, for example, help to imbue them with potent symbolic value. Art forms such as the masks used in ritual performances are highly symbolic. Whenever the well-being of a community is disrupted, or when a new situation is beginning (e g the initiation of a traditional diviner), the societal group in question sits down together to share a common meal. The spirit members of their society, the ancestors, are always included. This is a highly symbolic expression of community solidarity.

In Western Christian societies the cross is a symbol with continuing value. There are others as well: a wedding ring; a family sitting down together for the evening meal; a gift, however small, given and received. The possibilities are endless if people would only make an effort to reimbue their activities with symbolic purpose and meaning.

TRADITIONAL VERSUS WESTERN DOCTORS

It may be true that crises in African traditional societies occur less frequently and life is therefore more predictable than in the ultramodern world on which humankind has been launched. Nevertheless, when people in traditional communities face a personal crisis, they too seek help, not only from the community at large but from specialists, appointed and accepted by the spiritual as well as the visible members of the community. These specialists are the traditional doctors or diviners. Either a man or a woman may be chosen for this task of mediating health to individuals and thus to the visible community. In many respects, these persons may be compared to the shaman figure, which has become a subject for research among scholars of primal religions worldwide.

The traditional doctor deals with the crisis not only by treating the observed or acknowledged problem at surface level, but by probing more deeply to find the underlying spiritual cause. By thus seeking a reason, an answer to the question, 'why', he or she enables the patient to deal with the crisis more effectively.

In traditional societies, then, the sufferer is treated in a holistic manner, as if the body, the psyche and, in fact, the entire society were suffering by extension. Although there is a theoretical movement towards holistic medicine among modern medical practitioners, in actual practice people are still sent from one specialist to another. Each one observes, comments and prescribes on the basis of one aspect of the problem which he, and he alone, fully understands. Such an approach denies the fact that we are whole people. Our physical body is not an entity independent of our spiritual being.

Modern people have a need to be healed of the diseases which threaten to destroy humankind. There is a need for healing which includes both the physical and the spiritual dimension. There is a need for healing which enables people to recognise not only what they are, but what they are becoming as they face repeated crisis situations.

TEMPORAL ORIENTATION

In the Western world people have been schooled to think of time in linear terms as past, present and future, broken up into segments of hours, days, weeks, months and years. This is a very useful system for organising life in an industrialised society which prescribes times and places for productive work. In traditional African societies, however, time is not always conceived of in this way.

Various attempts have been made by Western scholars to express time as it is interpreted by Africans or other people from primal backgrounds. Cyclic time, for example, enables people to appreciate another way of viewing time's essence: seasons, celebrations and the like mark off one segment of time from another. Schilling (1973:120-147) deals, along with other important topics, with the relational character of time and the mystery which it offers the postmodern reader in his book, *The new consciousness in science and religion*.

An important contribution to the understanding of African temporal conceptions is made by Mbiti (1969:17) in a discussion of the Swahili words, zamani and sasa. Sasa represents a present 'now' period in which individuals live. Zamani is the distant past towards which we are all moving as we progress through the stages of life, from the sasa of our existence into the graveyard of time, the mythical past in which the ancestors dwell eternally. Both sasa and zamani have limited, built-in time structures as well. That is, the immediate temporal conception of sasa has a past, present and limited future, while there is a vague conception of distant past, more immediate past, and a possible future attached to the basically unlimited time of zamani. Life by and large moves backwards from a present sasa period into a past zamani, into which all eventually pass when they are forgotten after death.

The following excerpt from Turnbull's book on the Mbuti pygmies (1983:123) affords further insight into what an African conception of time may entail:

> One of the hunters cupped his hands into the form of a sphere and another pointed to the vaulted arch above us. From what followed it seemed that the Mbuti live not in a world of linear time and space, nor cyclical, but rather spherical. Ideally we should always be in the middle of our sphere. That is when there is *ekimi*. *Akimi* comes from moving away from the center of our sphere. This can be done by moving too fast, with violence, in body or mind. If we do that then we reach the edge of our sphere and it does not have time to catch up with us. Give it time, and it will, but meanwhile, in that world of time (and until time stops again?) we are *waziwazi*, a KiNgwana word that denotes complete disorientation and unpredictability. People who are *waziwazi* are best left well alone. Give them time, their spheres will catch up with them, they will be back in the center of the world and they will be all right. But if you are too violent or hasty (both among the most negative of values for the Mbuti) you may pierce the wall of your sphere. And as you pass through, like walking right into a river, something will come in and take your place in this world, as you enter the 'other' world. That person will look like you, but will not be you. So if someone is *waziwazi* for more than a few days, it is probably not that person at all, but his or her other self. Then it is best to move the camp and suggest that that person go off and join some other hunting band. Perhaps the real self will find a way back, for neither self likes to be in the wrong world.

Modern conceptions of rigidly linear time are being challenged as people move into outer space, discovering there the endless possibilities presented by the relativity of the two dimensions of time and space. Alvin Toffler (1983:307) illustrates the inadequacy of conventional concepts of time by suggesting that two people may see two bolts of lightning as having different time sequences. One person, standing beside a railway track, sees the two bolts strike simultaneously, one to the north, another to the south. The second person, who is travelling northward on a high-speed train, experiences the northern flash as occurring first and the one in the south, from which he is moving away, as occurring second. Time, then, is not absolute but relative to the velocity of the observer.

Thus Africans may, after all, be as accurate in their conceptions of time as Westerners. Certainly time conceptions in African cultures lend themselves to in-depth consideration. Consider the answer a Bushman is reported to have given when asked about his age. 'A man is as old as the number of disappointments he has known; a woman is as old as the number of lonely nights she has spent.' Or again, concerning beauty in a woman, 'A woman is beautiful when her eyes light up as her husband approaches, when her voice is warm as she answers his call, when the joy in her heart shines forth as he stands by her side'. A depth of insight is expressed here - insight not always to be found in our troubled society, oppressed by its consciousness of linear time and its enslavement to clocks and calendars.

Western people need to look again and to listen sympathetically to the religious experience of African people. Perhaps they can recapture something of the solidarity, the serenity and the healing which is needed for this 'now' generation. Mircea Eliade (1975:244-245) tells a beautiful story of a rabbi who sought a treasure in a far country by following directions he had received in a dream. Upon reaching his destination, he was met by an officer who laughed when the rabbi related his hopes and the message of the dream. 'I, too, had such a dream,' the officer replied, 'only I was urged to go to your house, where the treasure was hidden in a dusty corner behind an old stove. But I have no faith in such dreams'. The rabbi hurriedly returned, dug behind the stove in the dusty corner and there, sure enough, lay the treasure, awaiting discovery by the rabbi.

It may well be that people have, within their own heritage, the necessary healing for the ills of this modern world. But only by listening to the experiences of others will they know where to dig in order to find it.

Works consulted

Bailey, R C 1989. The Efe: archers of the African rain forest, in *National Geographic* 176 (5).

Beach, D N 1980. *The Shona and Zimbabwe 900-1850: an outline of Shona history.* New York: Africana.

Beier, U 1982. *Yoruba beaded crowns: sacred regalia of the Olokuku of Okuku.* London: Ethnographica.

Berglund, A-I 1976. *Zulu thought patterns and symbolism.* Cape Town: David Philip.

Biesele, M 1975. *Folklore and ritual of !Kung hunter-gatherers.* Cambridge, Mass: Harvard University (PhD thesis).

Biesele, M 1978. Religion and folklore, in *The Bushmen*, edited by P V Tobias. Cape Town: Human & Rousseau.

Bleek, D F (ed.) 1923. *The Mantis and his friends: Bushman folklore.* Cape Town: Maskew Miller.

Bleek, D F 1928. *The Naron: Bushman tribe of the central Kalahari.* Cambridge: Cambridge University Press.

Bourdillon, M F C 1976. *The Shona peoples.* Gwelo: Mambo Press.

Bryant, A T 1966. *Zulu medicine and medicine men.* Cape Town: Struik.

Callaway, H 1970. *The religious system of the Amazulu* (facsimile reprint). Cape Town: Struik. (First published 1870)

Daneel, M L 1970. *The God of the Matopo Hills: an essay on the Mwari cult in Rhodesia.* Mouton: The Hague.

Daneel, M L 1971. *The background and rise of southern Shona Independent Churches.* Mouton: The Hague.

Dupré, W 1975. *Religion in primitive cultures: a study in ethnophilosophy* Mouton: The Hague.

Eades, J S 1980. *The Yoruba today.* Cambridge: Cambridge University Press.

Eliade, M 1975. *Myths, dreams and mysteries.* New York: Harper Torchbooks.

Evans-Pritchard, E E 1956. *Nuer religion.* Oxford: Oxford University Press.

Ferguson, J 1970. *The Yorubas of Nigeria.* Bletchley, Buck: Open University Press.

Gelfand, M 1977. *The spiritual beliefs of the Shona.* Gweru: Mambo Press.

Gelfand, M 1981. *Ukama: reflections on Shona and Western cultures in Zimbabwe.* Gwelo: Mambo Press.

Hammond-Tooke, W D 1989. *Rituals and medicines: indigenous healing in South Africa.* Johannesburg: Ad Donker.

Hammond-Tooke, W D 1974. *The Bantu-speaking peoples of southern Africa.* London: Routledge & Kegan Paul.

Idowu, E B 1962. *Olodumare, god in Yoruba belief.* London: Longmans.

Jonas, P J & De Beer, F C 1988. *Socio-cultural anthropology (Study guide for SRA100-V).* Pretoria: Unisa.

King, N Q 1970. *Introduction to African religion.* London: Harper and Row.

Krige, E J 1950. *The social system of the Zulus.* Pietermaritzburg: Shuter & Shooter.

Kushner, L 1981. *The river of light: spirituality, Judaism, and the evolution of consciousness.* San Francisco: Harper & Row.

Lewis-Williams, D & Dowson, T 1989. *Images of power.* Johannesburg: Southern Book Publishers.

Lucas, J O 1948. *The religion of the Yorubas.* Lagos: CMS.

Maimela, S S 1985. Salvation in African traditional religions, in *Missionalia* 13 (2):63-77.

Marshall, L 1962. !Kung Bushman religious beliefs, in *Africa* 32 (3).

Mbiti, J S 1969. *African religions and philosophy.* New York: Frederick A Praeger.

Mbiti, J S 1970. *Concepts of God in Africa.* London: SPCK.

Mbiti, J S 1975. *Introduction to African religion.* London: Heinemann.

McClelland, E M 1982. *The cult of Ifa among the Yoruba.* London: Ethnographica.

Ngubane, H 1977. *Body and mind in Zulu medicine: an ethnography for health and disease in Nyuswa-Zulu thought and practice.* London: Academic Press.

Parrinder, G 1953. *Religion in an African city.* London: Oxford University Press.

Parrinder, G 1968. Traditional religions and modern culture (Africa), in *Proceedings of the XIth International Congress of the International Association for the History of Religions.* Leiden: E J Brill.

Parrinder, G 1969. *West African religion: a study of the beliefs and practices of Akan, Ewe, Yoruba, Ibo, and kindred people.* London: Epworth.

Ray, B C 1976. *African religions: symbols, ritual and community.* Englewood Cliffs: Prentice-Hall.

Schapera, I 1930. *The Khoisan peoples of South Africa.* London: Routledge & Kegan Paul.

Schilling, H K 1973. *The new consciousness in science and religion.* London: SCM.

Setiloane, G M 1976. *The image of God among the Sotho-Tswana.* Rotterdam: A A Balkema.

Setiloane, G M 1986. *African theology: an introduction.* Johannesburg: Skotaville.

Shooter, J 1857. *The Kafirs of Natal and the Zulu country.* London: Stanford.

Singer, R 1976. The biology of the San, in *The Bushmen*, edited by P V Tobias. Cape Town: Human & Rousseau, p 115-129.

Soyinka, W 1976. *Myth, literature and the African world.* Cambridge: University Press.

South African Museum 1976. *The Bushmen.* Cape Town: Rustica.

Taylor, J V 1963. *The primal vision: Christian presence amid African religion.* London: Heinemann.

Taylor, J & Van der Post, L 1984. *Testament to the Bushmen.* Middlesex: Viking.

Tempels, P 1959. *Bantu philosophy.* Paris: Presence Africaine.

Tobias, P 1976. *The Bushmen.* Cape Town: Human & Rousseau.

Toffler, A 1983. *The third wave.* London: Pan Books.

Turnbull, C 1961. *The forest people.* New York: Simon & Schuster.

Turnbull, C 1983. *The Mbuti pygmies: change and adaptation.* New York: Holt, Rinehart & Winston.

Twesigye, E D 1987. *Common ground: Christianity, African religion and philosophy.* New York: Peter Lang.

Van der Post, L 1961. *The heart of the hunter.* London: Hogarth.

Van Warmelo, N J 1974. The classification of cultural groups, in *The Bantu-speaking peoples of southern Africa,* edited by W D Hammond-Tooke, London: Routledge & Kegan Paul.

Vinnicombe, P 1976. *People of the eland: rock paintings of the Drakensberg Bushmen as a reflection of their life and thought.* Pietermaritzburg: University of Natal Press.

Woodhouse, B 1984. *When animals were people.* Mellville: Van Rensburg.